He is everything to me

The Lord is my Shepherd;
I shall not want.
He makes me lie down in green pastures:
He leads me beside still waters.
He restores my soul:
He leads me in paths of righteousness
for his name's sake.
Even though I walk through
the valley of the shadow of death,
I fear no evil:
For thou art with me;
thy rod and thy staff,
they comfort me.
Thou preparest a table before me
in the presence of my enemies:
thou anointest my head with oil;
my cup overflows.
Surely goodness and mercy shall follow me
all the days of my life:
and I shall dwell in the house of the Lord
forever.

He is everything to me

an exposition of Psalm 23

Ian Barclay

Charles Scribner's Sons • New York

1 3 5 7 9 11 13 15 17 19 C/P 20 18 16 14 12 10 8 6 4 2

Printed in the United States of America
Library of Congress Catalog Card Number 75-29735
ISBN 0-684-14543-X

Contents

Foreword

They say that to know and appreciate a person influences one's judgement of any book he may write, and in the present case this may well be so, for it has been my happiness to benefit from Ian Barclay's friendship over a good many years now. Nevertheless it is only one of the things which make me want to write in warm commendation of this study of Psalm 23.

In the summer of 1971 I heard some fragments of this book used in the ministry at the Southern Counties Christian Convention at Weston-super-Mare. It was clearly evident that God used His truth to bless and uplift His people. Today I have read through the complete manuscript at a single sitting and, without any sense of surprise, I find my heart enlarged with a fresh sense of love for the Lord Jesus and for His word. I am certain that this will be the experience of every reader.

Psalm 23 is a favoured portion of the word of God. Left to itself it breathes into the reader's spirit the calm and sense of security of which it speaks. It is beyond question a central word for today. In the rush and pressing anxieties of the world the people of God need above all the ministry of strengthening comfort. With many an apt illustration, with illuminating explanations and direct applications, Ian Barclay brings the ministry of comfort home. Fidelity to the word of God and care for the people of God combine in a book which God will surely bless and use.

Trinity College,
Stoke Hill,
Bristol

Alec Motyer
March 1972

Introduction

He is everything to me is the title of a song composed by Ralph Carmichael for the Billy Graham film 'The Restless Ones'. It exactly sums up the twenty-third psalm. As we shall see, David finds in God all that is necessary for a completely satisfying physical, emotional and spiritual life. You could slightly lengthen the title if you wished because since David wrote the psalm so many people have discovered that this psalm exactly meets their need. So you could call the psalm 'He is everything to *everybody*'.

Before me as I write is a scrapbook belonging to Mr F. D. Bacon. Mr Bacon is in his eighty-eighth year. He started work in an insurance office in the City of London at the age of fifteen. He is a Vice-President of the Crusaders Union and was a council member of the Scripture Union. Mr Bacon has kept a scrapbook on the twenty-third psalm since 1930, and it is full of different versions and paraphrases, clearly making the point that he is *everything to everybody*. There are over seventy versions in the scrapbook; there is the Japanese version; the City man's version; also, the cynic's, the heroin-taker's, the housewife's and the Sunday School teacher's. There are paraphrases by Red Indians, pilots, theologians and Trades Union members; there are dialect versions used by the Lowland Scots, the Scouse of Liverpool, the inhabitants of Kent and Sussex. The list is almost endless. Whatever your occupation, if you have experienced David's God, then you should be able to sit down and write your own version of the psalm.

I am grateful to the Billy Graham Evangelistic Association for permission to use the title of Ralph Carmichael's song as the title of this book.

St. Helen's   Ian Barclay
Bishopsgate,
London

'The Lord is my Shepherd'
Psalm 23:1

A Breath of Fresh Air

The picture of God shepherding his people is something that we would expect to find in a country where sheep play such an important part in the economy, and there is evidence that such language was used from the earliest times by the people of the Old Testament. When Jacob called down the blessing of God on his grandsons, he referred to a God who had 'led' him through life; and the word he used means 'shepherded' (Genesis 48·15). It was clearly Jacob's hope that the God who had shepherded him through life would now help the youngest members of his family. However, it could well be that when David refers to God directly as 'Shepherd' he is saying something that had never been said before.

In the first line of this psalm, when David exclaims *'The Lord is my Shepherd'*, he is using two sharply contrasting words for God. The first, 'Jehovah', which we translate as 'Lord', is the name for God which appears many more times than any other name for God in the Old Testament. Scholars agree that it is linked with the verb 'to be' and that it suggests that God is, he was, and he always will be with his people.

The second word, 'Shepherd', gives a totally different concept of God. For to call the great Jehovah-God a shepherd is as startling as Jesus calling God 'Abba, Father!' in the New Testament (Mark 14·36). For generations, God's people had been talking about the Fatherhood of God; then suddenly his name became one that any family would use. God became related to everyday life; he impinged on the personal; *Father* became *Dad* – for that is really what *Abba* means.

In Old Testament terms, David is saying the same sort of thing. Jehovah, the great *I am*, had suddenly become personal. When David said 'The Lord is my Shepherd' he must have startled his followers, for it was a statement of a radically new theology.

Creed into a conviction

No one knows when this psalm was written, yet some of the commentators try to set it into an historical setting. There is the recurring suggestion that it was written while David was experiencing some sort of hardship or exile. Both Dr. Kirkpatrick[1] in 1891 and Professor Blaiklock[2] in 1970 set it in the context of Absalom's rebellion (2 Samuel 15-17). The truth that David states in this psalm will fit into any part of his adult life. Therefore, it will do no harm for the purpose of this study to put it into this contest.

Before this period in his life, David had married Maacha, daughter of the King of Geshur. It had been a polygamous marriage, apparently for political reasons. The marriage produced the extremely handsome but rebellious Absalom who, for a good deal of his early adult life, plotted against his father. His chance really came when he took four hundred men to Hebron, ostensibly to attend a religious festival. At Hebron we are told that the hearts of the people of Israel went out to Absalom. David knew that Jerusalem, with its vulnerable water supply, was no city in which to endure a siege; so he immediately ordered his family and bodyguard to flee with him.

As far as an escape route was concerned, there was little choice open to David. Hebron, where Absalom was, lay twenty miles due south of Jerusalem. The foothills of the Shephelah leading on to the western plain would not offer enough cover for a man whose previous fighting experience had been in the comfortable security of the hills of Judah. If he kept to the hills and went northwards, through Ephraim towards Israel, he would have the menace of being surrounded by people whose loyalty he could not trust. That only left the hills of Gilead to the north east, which would mean going down into the rift valley and crossing the scorching heat of the plain of Jericho. David's objective there was Mahanaim, one of the principal towns of Gilead. Allowing for three companies of mercenaries, plus the family and servants, it must have been a group of nearly a thousand people which hurriedly left Jerusalem with David.

Jordan's Jungle

It would have been well into the second day when David arrived at the river Jordan, swiftly making its way down through the rift valley. The Jordan itself was no real barrier, but the *Zor*, what Jeremiah called Jordan's jungle (Jeremiah 12.5) which grew along the banks of the Jordan, was always formidable.

The extreme heat acted just like a greenhouse on the vegetation, causing the flowers to grow quickly to knee height and the grass to shoulder height. The whole area was a tangled mass of thorn, cane and oleander. To look down on the *Zor* from the surrounding hills was to see a twisting snake of vegetation following the banks of the Jordan.

But the real difficulty was not hacking a path through the *Zor* nor crossing the swift-flowing Jordan; it was doing both at speed, because Absalom was never very far behind.

Apart from the physical difficulties in which David found himself, it seems that his spiritual state was also precarious. There is plenty of evidence from the condition of David's court – intrigues, a polygamous marriage to someone outside the faith, a palace full of concubines – to suggest that the intimacy with which he had known God in his youth had slowly slipped away. Perhaps one reason was that he was now king. There were no Goliaths to fight, and he did not have to ask God for protection and provision for his flock. If he had a personal wish he simply asked a servant. If there were battles to be fought he sent a detachment of soldiers. Now rich in worldly wealth, his spiritual experience had run dry. It was years since he had used his remarkable ability for putting spiritual experiences into song. It could well be that over the last twenty years he had only written one psalm – that psalm of repentance after the sad affair with Bathsheba; and he would not have written that if his conscience had not been firmly prodded by the prophet Nathan (2 Samuel 12·7).

However, a change was taking place. Wading through the Jordan, getting scratched by the briars of the Zor, with the wonders of creation about him during the day, the infinity of the universe above him during the night, his mind was flooded with the spiritual recollections of his youth. As king he had just lost everything. It was no use appealing to his servants for help. But there was the God who had met his need in such a practical way when he was young. Sweating with the unaccustomed physical effort and the burning heat of the Jericho plain, David suddenly straightened his back and said 'God my Shepherd!' What had become a creed over the past few years since Absalom was born, once again became a conviction. Straight away, a new song begins to form in David's mind. He was still looking for a melody, but the two words Jehovah and Shepherd had emerged as the basis of a new psalm.

A new unity

Other things were happening too. What two days ago had been a conglomeration of people of different races and social positions was now welded into a group with a new loyalty. David had told the soldiers who formed his body-guard that there was no need for them to get mixed up in what was a family quarrel. He had pointed out that he could no longer promise the comforts of the palace barracks, and that in all probability they would not see their pay. David had said all this to the leader of the six hundred Gittites, the largest company of the mercenaries that had accompanied him from Jerusalem. Ittai replied, with one of the most astonishing statements of loyalty to be found in any literature: 'As the Lord lives, and as the lord my king lives, wherever the lord my king shall be, whether for death or for life, there also will your servant be' (2 Samuel 15.21). David had not only rediscovered a personal faith, but he had also discovered the secret of unity. There was no human uniformity in the group that fled with the king from Absalom's coup d'état. There was still a monarch and a royal family, mercenaries and servants: different social positions remained. Nor had individual identity been lost – there were still Israelites, Cherethites, Pelethites, Gittites among his followers. However, a common cause now overrode their differences. David found that unity did not come about by altering outward appearances, but by discovering a new commitment to each other because of a common cause. This unity was durable because it existed in spite of outward differences.

Dial mine, mine, mine

David said 'God *my* Shepherd'. This phrase not only implies David's new experience of God, but also his new relationship with him. Throughout the psalm, David refers to God thirteen times, and to himself seventeen times. To look at F. D. Bacon's scrapbook[3], which contains over seventy different paraphrases of the twenty-third psalm, is to see how easy it is to apply this psalm to any human situation. On the inside cover of the scrapbook is the date 1930, and four other words: *Dial Mine, Mine, Mine*. That is what David had done: he had made Jehovah his.

Dr Leslie Weatherhead tells that delightful story of the two ministers on a walking holiday in Snowdonia who came across a young shepherd boy. They wanted to tell him something of their faith, but they found that they did not have the vocabulary with which to communicate with a shepherd boy – until they remembered the twenty-third psalm. Taking the young boy's left hand they taught him five words one on each of the fingers: '*The Lord is my Shepherd*'. Within those five words the young boy seemed to understand the essence of a personal faith. When the two ministers returned for their annual holiday the following year, they spent a whole day looking for the young boy, wanting to know if he had grasped enough of the truth to sustain him during the intervening time. At dusk they had to give up their search, and they decided to walk down the mountains to their hotel. On the way they passed a cottage, and being extremely thirsty they went into the cottage to ask for a drink. There on the mantelpiece was a picture of the shepherd boy whom they were looking for. They explained that they wanted to see the young man. His mother said that that would not be possible, because he had died rather tragically in a storm the previous winter. She went to on say that she was still puzzled by the attitude in which his body had been found. His right hand had been clutching the third finger of his left hand. The ministers explained that the previous summer they had taught him five words on that left hand, and that at the moment of death the boy had been showing his trust in God. By clutching the third finger he was saying 'The Lord is *my* Shepherd'[4].

1. *Psalms, Vol.1*, by Dr. A.F. Kirkpatrick,
   Cambridge University Press, page 124.
2. *Psalms of the Great Rebellion*, by Prof. E.M. Blaiklock,
   Lakeland, page 16.
3. *Introduction*, page 8
4. *A Shepherd Remembers*, by Leslie Weatherhead,
   Hodder and Stoughton, page 32.

'I shall not want'
Psalm 23·1

Beds, Basins and Beans

It is so easy to think of David as one of the spiritual élite, and to imagine him enjoying a continual mountain-top experience of God, exclaiming 'The Lord is my Shepherd!'; and to conclude therefore that a similar experience will never be ours. We think this simply because we appear to live in spiritual valleys rather than hills. So if the historical background suggested in the previous chapter is true, it is helpful to note that David was both physically and spiritually at the bottom of a valley – and yet he could still say 'The Lord is my Shepherd!' The melody was returning to his life and he was beginning to write a psalm again.

Nevertheless, his situation had not changed. He had not been able to alter what had happened: the coup d'état had still taken place, and he was always conscious of being hardpressed by Absalom. Even though he had found the opening words of a new song, there was still no food with which to feed his soldiers and family, or tents for them to bivouac in at night. And as he reached Mahanaim, in the hills of Gilead, he could easily have realised the irony of this situation. The first person to speak of God shepherding his people was Jacob, and when Jacob came to Mahanaim an army of angels ministered to his need! For David, one ministering angel would have been enough. In the event, God sent three.

Two sides of the same coin

Perhaps the first thing that David noticed was a cloud of dust on the horizon that grew until he could distinguish three riders. They were Shobi, Machir and Barzilai. They

> 'brought beds, basins, and earthen vessels, wheat, barley, meal, parched grain, beans and lentils, honey and curds and sheep and cheese from the herd, for David and the people with him to eat; for they said, "The people are hungry and weary and thirsty in the wilderness." '
> (2 Samuel 17·27 ff).

The three riders brought all that David needed. He now had a few more words of his psalm; the words '*The Lord is my Shepherd*' were now balanced with '*I shall not want*'. In fact, the new words are only another way of expressing the first five, as the two phrases represent two sides of the same coin: the Jehovah God is the God who provides because he is the Shepherd. The first phrase represents the name of God in theological terms; the second, God as practically experienced by man. To talk about Jehovah as the Shepherd God is to speak about his character; to talk about the way that he provides for our needs is to describe the behaviour that is exactly appropriate to that character.

I once asked three young advertising artists to make a missionary display for Rochester Cathedral. They chose to do it on the history and work of the South American Missionary Society. They wanted the society's name to be as eye-catching as possible, so they decided to make the initials SAMS out of large, twelve-inch-high cork letters. The display was to be put in place on a Saturday and on the Friday one of the artists, Mike Shennon, went to buy the cork letters, only to be told that they were out of stock. He said that it was a matter of some urgency – but to emphasise her point the girl in the shop said, 'we only have the samples left', and put them on the counter. Mike Shennon looked down at the four sample letters. They spelled SAMS.

God's provision is often exactly what is necessary. David at Mahanaim got all that he wanted, from beds and basins to beans.

Angels unaware

It is not too far-fetched to suggest that Shobi, Machir and Barzilai were three over-laden *angels* when they met David at Mahanaim. *Angel* is a word that we frequently find in the Old and New Testaments, and it simply means a *messenger of God*. The word can be used to describe the vast army of heavenly creatures who surround God; equally it can be used to describe those human beings whom God chooses for his service. Of the many times that the Hebrew word is used in the Old Testament, nearly half are translated as *messengers*; for the rest, the word *angel* is used. Just how human the messengers could be can be seen from Malachi 3·1. The prophecy refers to John the Baptist when it says 'Behold, I send my messenger to prepare the way before me'. So Shobi, Machir and Barzilai were clearly God's *angels* when they brought all the material provision needed for David and his people.

Just how notable God's provision was for David at Mahanaim can be seen if we compare it with the classic biblical example of God's provision: the story in 1 Kings 17 of Elijah at the brook Cherith.

The unexpected place

Elijah was told by God to get away from the main thoroughfare of life and to hide himself at the source of the brook Cherith. There is always the feeling, conscious or subconscious, that it is easier for God to provide for our needs if we are in a familiar place and surrounded by people that we know. Behind this feeling is the belief that it is man, not God, who answers our prayers. This is like the little boy at Christmas who, having quietly thanked God in his bedtime prayers for all the blessings of the day, suddenly looks up at the ceiling, and with a loud voice cries 'Please God, can I have a bicycle for Christmas?' His mother says, 'Quietly, dear: God isn't deaf'. 'No, but Granny is,' declared the boy.

It is God who answers our prayers, and the place in which we find ourselves in no way hinders his ability to provide. We may be alone in a bed-sitter, cut off from friends and family, or alone in a strange country, cut off by the barriers of language. In either case, we are no further away from God's help than we are at any other time. I had a letter from a missionary not long ago who had been on holiday in India. When it was time to return to Thailand where she was working she had to make the long overnight journey from Hazaribagh to Calcutta. Armed with instructions on what to do when she got to Calcutta, she set off. Her letter continues:

'Maybe I dozed a little as the train clattered on its way – I don't clearly remember. What I do remember, though, is opening my purse near the end of the journey and finding that nearly all my money was missing. At first I felt numb. Then I was seized with panic: how was I going to complete the journey from Calcutta station to my destination several miles away? I did not know Calcutta and I could not speak the language. In my desperation, I prayed.

As I bundled myself and three large cases out of the train, coolies sprang up all round me wanting to carry my cases, but I knew I couldn't pay them; so, to their anger and bewilderment, I struggled on alone. At the barrier I had to put one bag down in order to get through the turnstile. Suddenly a brown hand grabbed it and hurried off. I followed in quick pursuit. The man with my case turned round and in very good English said 'You'll need a taxi. You have to fight for them here; I'll get one for both of us.' All sorts of terrible thoughts rushed through my mind of what might happen to a girl who went off in a taxi with a strange man.

The taxi ride seemed endless. How could I tell the man that I hadn't enough money to pay my share of the fare? Rather lamely I began, "I feel I ought to pay my share, but . . . " He cut me short: "No, no" he said, "you are a guest in my country. I am a Christian and I would like to do this for you".'

God can quite clearly provide for us in the most unexpected place.

Improbable means

It is clear that God can also provide by the most improbable means. For Elijah, God chose ravens to airlift in bread and meat twice a day to where the prophet was tucked away in a spiritual cul-de-sac at the source of the brook Cherith. The particular species of ravens referred to were meat eaters, so they were much more likely to eat the meat than to deliver it. They were also notorious for not looking after their own young, therefore the regularity with which they looked after Elijah is again quite remarkable.

During World War 2, by equally improbable means, God provided for Mrs Harrison Dulles, sister-in-law of the American diplomat. In January 1943 Mrs Dulles was living at Villars de Lans near Grenoble with her young son Billy, who was ill with pneumonia. One evening she was disturbed by loud banging at the villa door. Mrs Dulles, not easily intimidated, was forced by the officer of a German patrol to dress. She was told to dress her young son too, unless she wanted to carry him almost naked from the building. Because of his high temperature, Billy was dressed with extra clothing and wrapped in a blanket before he was carried downstairs by his mother to a waiting lorry, which drove them towards the mountains. It was a clear night; snow was on the ground. The dark sky was pierced with the light of a million stars. The lorry stopped. Mrs Dulles and

Billy were ordered out and the German patrol followed them as they struggled through the snow. She began to stagger, trying to hold a heavy child. Then she could carry him no longer, and he slowly slid to his feet to walk at her side. She prayed.

'Halt!'

They had come to the mountainside and a rocky overhang caused the officer's order to echo over the white fields. As they stood there snow began to fall again. With a pistol in his hand the officer directed his patrol to line up opposite the mother and child, and to load their rifles.

'Have you no children of your own? I beg you, free the boy. We are both innocent, but he is a mere child. You cannot do this,' Mrs Dulles pleaded with the German officer.

'I have children, but what does that matter?'

There was no feeling in the officer's eyes as he spoke. He ordered the woman and child to stand up straight and turn towards his patrol. Billy's head protruded from the blanket as he said:

'Mother, look up at the lovely stars. God is not asleep yet. He is watching us.'

Sixty seconds of silence followed before the night was shattered by the officer's voice ordering his men to lower their rifles and to dismiss. He turned to Mrs Dulles and said:

'Yes, I too have children. You are free.'

A few minutes later the soldiers drove off in their lorry, leaving Mrs Dulles and Billy to walk home to their villa through the snow. A young boy with pneumonia who saw the stars was the means by which God provided an answer to an American woman's prayer.

Remarkable abundance

In a very lonely place, with ravens as delivery boys, God provides for Elijah with remarkable abundance. Twice a day the ravens deliver bread and meat for the prophet. God's provision is often staggering because of its abundance. This is not merely a feature of Old Testament teaching; at the wedding reception at Cana in Galilee Jesus made no less than one hundred and eighty gallons of wine. The same superabundance of provision has been seen down the ages of the church until our own time.

Dr D. Vaughan Rees tells us of God's provision in modern times when he writes about the Ye-Su Chia-ting (The Jesus Family) in Communist China. In 1948 communist pressure forced the Overseas Missionary Fellowship to close its hospital at Honan. Dr Vaughan Rees was asked to go to the northern province of Shantung, but soon after his arrival the Bamboo Curtain came down and he was compelled to stay in China for the next two years. In the end Dr Vaughan Rees applied for a pass to leave. When he had originally made his application to the communists he had mentioned the fact to a Miss Helen Tso that he had no western clothes and could scarcely go abroad in Chinese dress. She told him not to worry, taking a measuring tape from her pocket to measure him. The Doctor asked if she had ever made a Western suit. Miss Tso replied that she had not, but she did not foresee any difficulty if she could find a photograph of one in a magazine.

Four months after the application an exit pass was suddenly granted to Dr Vaughan Rees. He had resigned himself to wearing Chinese clothes after he left. However, his original anxiety proved groundless, because the day before he was to leave China, Miss Tso arrived with *three Western suits with shirts and ties to match, plus socks, shoes and an overcoat.* Later when Dr Vaughan Rees examined his suits he found that the right colour handkerchief had been put in the breast pocket of each.

'What will I say to the communists when they examine my bags?' asked the Doctor.

'Say that they were all made from rich material from the Chinese gowns which people discarded when they wanted to wear the poor material of the other members of the Jesus Family,' was Miss Tso's full reply. And this is the way that Dr Vaughan Rees describes the overcoat in his book:

> 'The overcoat is a masterpiece; it is lined with astrakhan, and has a fur collar. It is rather too ornate to wear at home, as it also has an inside silk covering, similar to the best tailored Chinese coats[1].'

Over-awed by spiritual giants

It is so easy to be over-awed by the story of someone like Dr Vaughan Rees. In fact, he warns against this in the introduction to his book, emphasising that he is just an ordinary Christian man. Stories like that of David's conflict with Goliath can also easily make us feel over-awed, but a fuller study will reveal that David was not only a 'military genius, a king whose name is carved in world history,' but that he was also 'bitter, insecure, resentful, the child of a divided home . . . pop star, the idol of every girl of the land . . . a homeless vagrant playing hide-and-seek with death[2].' The same is true of Elijah as James emphasises when he says 'he was perfectly human as we are' (James 5·17 Living Bible). What has been given us in the Bible are not the stories of what God can do for great men, but what a great God has done for very ordinary people.

Ultimately, for Dr Vaughan Rees in China, for Elijah at the source of the brook Cherith, for David at Mahanaim it was not the gifts that were important, but the experience of the Giver. If the Lord is our Shepherd we shall not want. But if we grasp, we will only get a human-sized handful of provision. A little boy was once helping a farmer pick some strawberries, and as a reward the farmer invited him to keep a handful for himself. The boy hesitated for a moment and then said, 'Please may it be *your* hand?' How wise he was. There is similar spiritual wisdom in looking at the Giver rather than the gifts.

Strange bedfellows

In a biblical sense Shobi, Machir and Barzilai were certainly God's *messengers*. They provided all that David needed for his family and men. Shobi was a foreigner, an Ammonite, one of the traditional and cruel enemies of God's people. He was the son of Nahash who had befriended David. The home of Nahash was the city of Rabbah, situated twenty-three miles east of the Jordan at the head waters of the Jabbock. The fact that God used Shobi raises in our minds all the problems of receiving help from the enemies of God's people. That General Booth, after receiving a donation from the infamous Marquess of Queensberry, said 'We will wash it in the tears of the widows and orphans and lay it on the altar of humanity' has never really convinced me, and I confess I cannot understand why Shobi was used.

Machir was a loyal friend; loyal to the king, whoever that was. He had been loyal to Saul's family by looking after Mephibosheth at Lodebar and he could be trusted to be loyal to David.

Barzilai was a rich Gileadite, and no one will ever know how much the church owes to the Barzilais of every generation.

The problem is, how, just how, did these three particular gentlemen find themselves riding together? I suppose the only answer is that the God who can provide with a variety that extends from beds and basins to beans can also send the provision by a variety of delivery boys.

1. *The Jesus Family in Communist China* by Dr Vaughan Rees, Paternoster, page 40.
2. *David* by John Hercus, IVP, cover.

'He makes me lie down in green pastures.
He leads me beside still waters'
Psalm 23·2

The Cool Waters of the Wadi Fara

If it had not been for an article in *The Times* for August 11th 1955, I would not have known very much of the background to the green pastures and still waters of this second verse. What really caught my attention was the first sentence of the article which said that *the still waters of the twenty-third psalm had proved comfort to more souls than any other spring in history*. Knowing the accuracy of *The Times*, I felt compelled to read on. The article said that the location of the verse was not difficult to discover because the Wadi Fara was the only valley in the hill country of Judaea that had green pastures and still waters. The Wadi Fara was described as a broad, fertile valley, nine miles north east of Jerusalem, running down to the plain of Jericho.

Until 1926 the wadi was only frequented by hermits and shepherds, and was the home of porcupines and rabbits. In 1926 a severe drought deprived Jerusalem of its only piped water supply from Solomon's pool; so, as an emergency operation, the spring of Wadi Fara was brought into use. Nine years later, a new scheme for bringing plenty of water from the ancient city of Antipatris was completed, so the spring at Wadi Fara was abandoned.

Trouble arose again in 1948 when the truce line divided Jerusalem, leaving the whole of the water supply on the Israeli side. The only solution was to re-open the pipe line to the spring at Wadi Fara which had been closed in 1935. However, the spring was known to yield only 300,000 gallons of water a day, and the authorities realized that this amount of water would hardly supply the needs of the 90,000 inhabitants of old Jerusalem plus the inhabitants of the growing township of Ramallah. To show how the problem was solved, let me quote the exact words from *The Times*; for it was solved 'by phenomena wholly in tradition with the Land of the Book. The yield of the spring, which was never known to vary, whether in drought or flood, suddenly doubled. It has remained constant ever since[1]'.

Spiritual satisfaction

Sheep graze from 3.30 am until 10 am and then lie down for about four hours' rest, chewing their cud and putting on fat. The shepherd has to start very early in the morning, leading his flock through the rough herbage to the tender grasses; finally the flock is brought to a shady place with the sweetest grasses of all where the sheep lie down in contentment.

The marginal reading for this verse allows 'tender grasses'; that is, young grasses, sweet grasses, the first shoots of vegetation. The shepherd also leads the flock to still waters. Sheep are frightened by fast-moving water; if they fall into a spring, the weight of water absorbed by their woollen coats can prevent them from climbing out; and consequently they drown. Fear of water is therefore deeply inbred into sheep as a species, and so the shepherd always has to look for a place where rock erosion has caused a quiet backwater where they can drink without fear. These are not stagnant waters; they are fresh, refreshing, gentle waters, still enough to cause no anxiety to the sheep.

Spiritual bankruptcy

The verse that we are looking at speaks of spiritual refreshment. It shows that God was looking after David in the way that he used to look after his sheep. As David had made sure that his flock was satisfied, so God satisfied David. Yet today so few Christians appear to be spiritually satisfied. The other day I came across a letter from Philip Doddridge to Isaac Watts, the great hymn writer of the eighteenth century. In it he says

> 'It is the unanimous Judgement of this church that the frequent acts of Bankruptcy which have happened in dissenting congregations elsewhere, have brought so great a Dishonour on Religion . . . that we are obliged in Duty to enter our publick protest and caution on this head. And we do hereby declare that if any person in stated communion with us shall become Bankrupt or as it is commonly expressed failed in the world, he must expect to be cut off from our Body . . . .'[2]

That is the strong way that Christians wrote to each other in the eighteenth century. Doddridge was obviously speaking about financial bankruptcy, but surely spiritual bankruptcy and spiritual failure brings an even greater dishonour upon our Christian faith.

By guess or by God

Perhaps the clue to our spiritual bankruptcy lies in the words 'he leads me'. In other words, the problem is not lack of spiritual refreshment; it is there, as it was for David, if only we can be led to it. Up to now we have seen verse 2 in its historical setting. We have also seen it in its pastoral setting: the flock, surrounded by tender grasses and quiet waters. But what is the practical setting? How can we be led to the completely satisfying spiritual refreshment that God offers his people today?

Surely the only answer to that must be by the Bible. I like the story that Charles Allen tells in his book on the twenty-third psalm about the president of the big American company who came to see him. The business man was a man of unusual ability and energy that had enabled him to achieve almost everything that he desired; only peace and happiness continued to elude him. Finally, his doctor suggested that he should talk to a minister. The man spoke to Charles Allen of all the prescriptions that the doctors had given him, and how they had failed to work. Let Charles Allen continue the story:

> 'Then I took a sheet of paper and wrote out my prescription for him. I prescribed the Twenty-third Psalm five times a day for seven days.
>
> I insisted that he take it just as I prescribed. He was to read it the first thing when he awakened in the morning – carefully, meditatively, and prayerfully. Immediately after breakfast, he was to do exactly the same thing; also immediately after lunch, again after dinner, and, finally, just before he went to bed.
>
> It was not to be a quick, hurried reading. He was to think about each phrase, giving his mind time to soak up as much of the meaning as possible. At the end of just one week, I promised, things would be different for him.'[3]

The twenty-third psalm, and the rest of the Bible, is the tender grass and the quiet water that God provides for our complete satisfaction: the Bible is the spiritual Wadi Fara. So let us try to analyse the exact nature of the spiritual pastures and to re-open that pipeline which has been the source of comfort to more people than any other spring in history.

God's brainwave

Paul tells Timothy that *'all scripture is inspired by God'* 2 Timothy 3·16. Not many people would disagree with that statement, for the Bible carries the stamp of great literature: clearly, the writers were *inspired* men. We use the word *inspired* to describe the creative process of a man: man sees a daffodil and is inspired to write a poem; or his mind is filled with music, which he feels he must write down. Equally, a disciple may have heard Jesus preach a sermon, or seen him heal the sick, and felt moved to write a gospel account. However, that is not what Paul is talking about to Timothy. The translator had to use the word *inspire* because there does not seem to be an English word for the creative process that Paul mentions here. For Paul is not talking about something coming into the mind of a man, but about something coming out of the mouth of God. A better translation would be 'all scripture is *breathed out* by God'.

Every Bible has on its spine more or less the same words: 'Holy Bible'. I would like to have those two almost meaningless words obliterated, and to have substituted the words that Bernard Miles uses for his Chilternian translation of some of the gospel stories; that is, *God's Brainwave*.[4] For that is exactly what the Bible is: it is God's brainwave. Not Isaiah's brainwave, or Matthew's or Mark's or Paul's; but God's.

I used to work for a firm of merchant bankers where I spent a few months in the base metal department, trading in tin, zinc and lead. A great deal of the world's metal ore is mined in Australia, from which had come one of the department's favourite stories. It was about an Australian farmer who owned a mountain. The ground of this vast area simply consisted of a few inches of infertile dust on solid bedrock, from which he could hardly produce enough food for his family, let alone enough to trade with in order to develop his business. So he went bankrupt. Another farmer bought the mountain and discovered that it was not rock that lay beneath the dust like soil, but *solid zinc ore*. The farmer who had gone bankrupt had been standing on a mountain of treasure.

Many people would describe their Bibles as the first farmer would have described his land: dry, arid and dusty. Indeed, it is true to say that when we hold a Bible in our hands we are only holding man-made paper, printed with man-made words with man-made printers' ink. But just below the surface is the most fantastic treasure: God's brainwave. The Bible may appear to be dry and dusty on the surface, but underneath is the food of the tender grasses and the cool water that God provides for his people.

The lively oracles of God

Green pastures and still waters meant fat sheep with heavy, luxuriant coats. It meant that they were satisfied, contented, willing to lie down for their full four hours' rest without wanting to get up to look for more food. At her Coronation Service the Queen was presented with a copy of the Bible, and she was told that the book contained *the lively oracles of God*. Dr E. V. Rieu, translator of the gospels into modern English for the Penguin Classic Series, said to J. B. Phillips, another distinguished modern translator, that his work had changed him because he had found the Bible *extraordinarily alive*[5]

The Rosetta stone

Paul says to Timothy that all scripture is inspired by God and 'is profitable for teaching'. The AV translates that last word as 'doctrine'. Thomas Carlyle's great cry was 'feed me on the facts'; and that is what the Bible does for us: it gives us the facts, the doctrine, the teaching in a language we can understand.

When the French army went down into Egypt under Napoleon, an engineer digging the foundations for army barricades came upon a stone which historians have called the 'Rosetta stone'. The stone contained a priestly proclamation in honour of Ptolemy V, written in three languages. The first two were known Egyptian languages which had previously proved beyond translation because there was no key to their hieroglyphics; the third was Greek, providing the long-awaited key. The discovery of the Rosetta stone led scholars into a new area of knowledge. The Bible is the Christian's Rosetta stone, written in words that we can understand so that we have the key to the great truths that have come from the mouth of God.

The design of truth

According to the Revised Standard Version, the next word that Paul uses is that the Bible is profitable for' reproof', which literally means 'to convince'. Paul is saying that the Bible can ensure our intellectual conviction.

The Bible's power to convince the mind can be seen in the history of the Christian church in Korea. The Koreans are a people with a very long history who have developed a culture of their own. Perhaps it was to preserve that culture that they became a hermit people, closing their country to all outsiders. Yet when the first missionaries arrived in the country in 1884, they found a handful of Christians.

Twenty years earlier the Rev. Robert Jermaine Thomas felt called to be a missionary in China. Almost immediately after their arrival his wife died in the most tragic circumstances. Some sort of holiday seemed right for Mr Thomas to adjust to his wife's death so, taking his supplies with him, he decided to travel to Korea on an American trading schooner called the *General Sherman*. As the schooner sailed up the Daidong River towards Pyengyang, the northern capital, it was caught on the mudflats. The Koreans, hostile to strangers, executed the passengers and crew; they then set the schooner alight having first taken the cargo ashore out of curiosity.

Korean houses, like most Oriental houses, have little furniture: but they have highly decorated walls. The rice paper of the Bibles found in the cargo holds of the schooner seemed just right for the wall decoration. No doubt it was the scholars who knew Chinese who appreciated the new wallpaper most; after all, through the design they were being fed the facts. And that handful of people were not only convinced, but also converted by reading their wall-paper.

God's moral hammer

The Bible also ensures our moral growth. Paul tells Timothy that the doctrine of the scriptures is profitable for 'correction'. Helmut Thielicke says 'The word of God is not a feast for our ears but a hammer,' and the force of the hammer to shape the lives of people even within our permissive society is often quite remarkable.

Take the story of a young lady in public relations with no Christian background. Christian friends invited her away for a small weekend houseparty where she was converted. The Word of God clearly became a living force in her life over the weekend. No one at the houseparty knew that she had been living with a young man called Tony for some years; but God spoke to her through his Word.

She returned to London, greeted Tony and went into the bathroom to get ready for bed. In her makeup bag was the month's supply of the Pill. Should she take just one more, and gently tell Tony that she'd become a Christian? After a moment's hesitation, there was no more indecision in her mind. She went into the kitchen, and down the waste disposal unit went the Pill. Straight away the relationship stopped. Such is the force of the hammer of the Word of God to correct our lives.

The young lady involved said to me in a letter shortly after the weekend, 'My chastity – this word, which previously held for me strong Victorian connotations has now revealed its true meaning – is a delight. It means that I am "whole for God".'

Equipped for every good work

Paul's final words to Timothy about the Bible are that it is used for 'training in righteousness, that the man of God may be complete, equipped for every good work.' Here is the assurance that the Bible can give us spiritual training, maturity and equipment. It is the map to the tender grasses and gentle waters of the spiritual Wadi Fara.

During the first World War the retreating French blew up a bridge over a deep river to hinder the advancing Germans. Yet the Germans marched straight across the river, to the astonishment of the bystanders. One of the German officers remembered an old book in which Caesar described his campaigns in Gaul. The Roman armies had crossed the river by a ford at exactly the same spot. The bridge had been standing for so many centuries that the ford had been completely forgotten.

In our own time many of the familiar bridges to spiritual maturity have been slowly removed; but the Bible is the old book which clearly maps the way.

Cooking your own goose

We have spent a whole chapter looking at the rich pastures of the people of God, and how they may be re-discovered today; but we have to be very careful about spiritual gluttony. The shepherd led his flock to the sweet grasses and quiet waters for a particular part of the day: they did not live there. There is a spiritual Wadi Fara from which we can get complete spiritual refreshment today. But we must not live there: having taken our refreshment we are to move out of the valley to live life for God.

1. Article from *The Times* of August 11th 1955.
2. *Isaac Watts – His Life and Works* by Arthur Paul Davis, Independent Press, page 48.
3. *The Twenty-Third Psalm* by Charles L. Allen, Fleming H. Revell, page 11.
4. *God's Brainwave* by Bernard Miles, Hodder and Stoughton.
5. *Layman's Answer* by E.M. Blaiklock, Hodder and Stoughton, page 44.
6. *The Waiting Father*, by Helmut Thielicke, Harper and Row, page 56.

'He restores my soul'
Psalm 23·3

This Perishing Thing is a Danger to Life

I had taken my car to the local garage to have a slow puncture repaired. When I called to collect it, the garage owner, Dan O'Kelly, was most apologetic. Holding an inner tube in his hand, he said,

'I'm afraid I have had to fit a new one; this one was so perished that it was dangerous.'

To my uninitiated, unmechanical eyes, the inner tube looked quite all right. But as soon as Dan O'Kelly began to stretch it, I saw that the rubber had lost its resilience and that it split easily. It was obviously not a question of adding one or two patches. The rubber had gone, and nothing could save it. In its present state, it was clearly a danger to life.

The same word that Dan O'Kelly used to describe the inner tube of my tyre is the word that the Bible uses to describe human life without God. It is *perishing*. It is not a case of adding one or two patches to life: a patch called *being good*, or slightly larger patch labelled *will try more next time*. The real problem is that the whole fabric of life is breaking up, and nothing can save it. We would think twice about setting out on a motorway with an inner tube in such a dangerous state, yet without a second thought we venture out on life unconcerned by the weaknesses in our character caused by trying to live without God.

A remarkable offer

If the Bible informs us that human life is perishing, then it goes on with the quite remarkable news that things can change. It offers us *new* life. In the dullness of the English language, it is not always obvious how remarkable this offer is. In the language of the New Testament there are two words for 'life'. The first is *bios* which refers to *biological* life. The second is *zoe*, which although sometimes used to describe natural, physical life, was much more often reserved to describe the *life force* in a man, or even God's life – the life of heaven. *Bios* was therefore more often used to describe the physical life, the length of time that we would spend on earth. When the New Testament offers us 'life', it is not *bios* but *zoe*. It is not saying that we can have more biological life; but it is saying that we can have God's life, or the life of God's heaven. And this life, to use another biblical word, is *imperishable* (1 Peter 1·4)

The offer accepted

In the opening words of verse 3, David deals with his own acceptance of this new life. David had been conscious that over the years he had drifted away from God. His life was disintegrating. His political career began to decline as soon as Absalom began to steal the hearts of the people of Israel from him (2 Samuel 15·6), and he must have felt that it was completely over when he had to retreat from an attack by his own son. David knew that his spiritual life had been a sham in recent years; as for his family life, Absalom was a constant reminder to him that no good could possibly come out of a marriage arranged for purely political reasons.

David's rediscovery of God, and of God's provision and refreshment, led also to the discovery of the way of restoration. There was no attempt on David's part to patch up his life. What had been wrong was taken away. The life that was perishing was replaced by the life that was imperishable. '*He restores my soul*' is the emphatic way that David puts it in this psalm. The Hebrew word for 'soul' is a synonym for the word 'me', so David is saying 'he restores me'. For David, restoration was as complete as that.

He causes my life to return

There are probably more variations in the translation of the first four words of this verse than any other four words in the whole psalm, which only emphasises the dramatic nature of David's restoration. Moffatt translates it 'he revives life in me'. The Book of Common Prayer, following the Greek version of the Old Testament, renders it 'he converts my soul'. Albert Barnes, writing at the end of the last century, said that these words can literally be translated 'he causes my life to return'.

This is a pointer to the restoration that is available to us. If we have never exchanged the old life for the new life that God offers us, then He can convert us. If we have merely drifted away from God over the years, then he can cause our life to return. If we have grown cold in spiritual things, then he can revive us. 'He restores me', says David. There is no limit to the kind of restoration that God can work in us. We simply have to discover the place where this restoration can take place.

A cross marks the spot

The death of Jesus is the event that completely restores a man. At the cross, the disintegrating human life is exchanged for the imperishable life of God. By the death of Jesus, man's failures are completely removed, and man's sins are entirely forgiven.

It may sound highly anachronistic to associate the death of Jesus with the restoration of a Judean king who lived almost exactly a thousand years earlier. But I do not think that it is. I do not even have to turn over a page in my Bible to link David's restoring experience of God with his experience of the cross of Jesus. The cross is in the previous psalm. We do not know, of course, if David fully understood all that he was writing about. Yet in Psalm 22 he foresees the crucifixion in a way that is decidedly uncanny if we do not accept that it was prophetic vision. David saw the death of Jesus.

Isn't this a bit far-fetched?

I confess that I am always sceptical when anyone tells me that a particular passage in the Bible obviously refers to something that happened a thousand years later. But it is very difficult not to see the death of Jesus in Psalm 22. You cannot say that David was describing the death of a criminal, who had been condemned to capital punishment, because the Hebrew form of capital punishment was death by stoning, not crucifixion.

Then the words that Jesus spoke on the cross are clearly the first and the last words of this psalm. '*My God, my God, why hast thou forsaken me?*' are the first words (Psalm 22·1, Matthew 27·46). While the last words are not in the same mood, they express exactly the same meaning and sense of achievement. '*He has done it*' says the psalm (Psalm 22·31, AV). '*It is finished*' says Jesus on the cross, and without straining the text at all this could easily read '*It is done*' (John 19·30).

Unhappy tree

It has been said that David in Psalm 22 describes the crucifixion more vividly than any of the gospel writers. The main figure in Psalm 22 says '*they have pierced my hands and my feet*' (verse 16). It is difficult to better his description of the position of someone hanging by his hands: '*I am poured out like water and all my bones are out of joint*' (verse 14). All he can see is his own ribcage, thrust forward: '*I can count all my bones*' (verse 17). The gaping crowd '*open wide their mouths*' (verse 13), criticising and gesticulating as they

44

'*make mouths at me*' and '*wag their heads*' (verse 7). He cried for a drink because '*my tongue cleaves to my jaws*' (15), and as he hangs on the cross all he can notice is the crowd's incredible insensitivity '*they divide my garments among them, and for my raiment they cast lots*' (verse 18).

David so very clearly foresaw the death of Jesus that there can be nothing accidental about the words in this psalm. It was part of the perfect planning of God.

From the black night to the golden day

The flag of Belgium was chosen to express a definite belief. It is a tricolour of the three colours black, red and gold. Its meaning is declared in the phrase '*de la nuit au jour par le sang*' (through blood we passed from the black night to the golden day). The flag was chosen as a perpetual reminder to the nation of those who had shed their blood so that Belgium could be a free country.

The phrase '*through blood we passed from the black night to the golden day*' exactly sums up David's experience of God. He was a restored man. From the night of disintegrating human experience without God, he had passed through blood to the light of God's golden day.

The Paul Temple affair

Among my earliest memories is an exciting weekly serial I used to listen to on radio. I only have to hear a piece of music called *Coronation Scot* to bring back a spine-chilling episode of the radio version of Paul Temple. At the time, I did not realise that I would meet the man who recorded that particular piece of theme music for the BBC. His name is Norton Colville.

Norton started his business life in the nineteen-twenties working in his father's engineering business, but he soon left to go into show business as a dance band leader. Norton Colville went into the first flight of dance band leaders in the nineteen-fifties. His band broadcast regularly, he had his own dancing school, and he also gave dancing lessons over the air in a BBC programme called *Club Piccadilly*, when he was accompanied by Steve Race and Malcolm Lockyer.

At the top, in spite of being successful and making a lot of money, Norton Colville found that things were going wrong. He was not happy. His marriage and his professional life began to disintegrate. On June 16th 1956 he decided to end it all. With sleeping tablets in his pocket he decided to go home and take his own life. While he was waiting for a tube at St John's Wood a group of young people came on to the platform singing. At first Norton Colville thought that they had been drinking, and then he was aware that they were singing a hymn. After they had boarded the tube, one of the group came to him and said,

'What do you think about Jesus Christ?'

Half an hour later the young man took Norton Colville into St Martin-in-the-Fields and quietly sitting in a pew showed him how to be forgiven. He had begun the day, conscious that the whole fabric of life was slipping from him. He could not hold on. So far as he was concerned, *the perishing thing was a danger to life*. He finished the day aware that *God had restored his soul*. Four months later, writing about his experience at St Martin-in-the-Fields, he said *'I surrendered my life to Christ. I knew that He had been to the cross and died for me'*. So definite was Norton Colville's restoration that he could add *'My life was completely changed. Old things had passed away, all things had become new'*.

Just as the restored David was used by God, so God used Norton Colville, who from that moment entered full-time Christian work.

Your saying so don't make it so

When Mark Twain was young he got into a fight with someone much bigger than himself. As a form of defence he suddenly said that he had a big brother. To which his

opponent wisely replied, '*Your saying so don't make it so.*'
Simply to be able to say, 'he restores my soul', doesn't
make it so! Nothing but the real experience of forgiveness
will change our perishing life into the imperishable life of
God.

'He leads me in paths of righteousness
for his name's sake.'
Psalm 23·3

Doing it His Way

The second part of verse 3 may appear to be simple, but once you try to analyse it you discover that it is far from easy to understand. However, there seem to be three separate strands of thought in these words.

Follow my leader

Firstly, we are told that the Shepherd guides us: '*he leads me*' is the way that David puts it in the psalm. This is not surprising as the eastern shepherd walked before his flock rather than behind as they do in western countries.

Secondly, we are told that the Shepherd guides us into '*paths of righteousness*'. It is very easy to get the wrong impression from these words because of the twentieth century meaning that we attach to them. John McNeill, the Scottish preacher, said that he always found it difficult to expound the word *paths* until he had visited South Africa. Preaching one day in a Dutch Reformed Church, with an Afrikaans Bible open before him on the pulpit desk, McNeill found verse three of the Psalm simply to see what it looked like. He saw:

> *Hy verkwik my siel; Hy lei my in*
> *die spore van geregtigheid, om sy*
> *Naam ontwil.*

The word *spore* caught his attention. He immediately remembered that when he was young he used to follow the

49

sheep's spoor or the *sheep's footprints* through the hills of his native Scotland.

The Shepherd does not guide us into paths of righteousness that are as well defined as the pavements of a European city. Rather he guides us to the place where we can find, with his wisdom, his clear imprint on the righteous way. To put it another way: we are to follow him. The second half of verse 3 is really a question of *follow my leader*.

Before we move on from this point we must look at the word *righteousness* because there is a chance that our understanding of this word has become overlaid with a meaning that David did not intend. Before the beginning of the sixteenth century this word was pronounced *rightwise*. In Old Testament times *righteous* was used to describe anything that was physically *right* or *correct*, such as the *just* weights of Deuteronomy 25·15. But it slowly came to mean all that was spiritually right. Righteousness was never meant to describe an exaggerated piety; the sort of behaviour that is so other-worldly that it is neither human nor bearable. The righteous life is the well-balanced life. To continue to enjoy that life we must follow the Shepherd, by living life *his way*.

Magnifying God

The *third* strand of thought in verse 3 is that God gains glory for himself when his people obey him. Just as a teacher's ability is declared by the success of his pupil and a doctor's success is measured by the health of his patient, so glory is given to God by the right behaviour of his people. David puts it like this, 'he leads me in paths of righteousness *for his name's sake*'. The names of God in the Bible are also descriptions of his character. In this Psalm David adds *shepherd* to the names of God that we already know. The man whose sheep were scattered over the foot hills of Lower Gilead was hardly worthy of the name shepherd; that name is reserved for a man who can skilfully keep his

flock intact as he leads them down on to the Plain of
Jericho, and then up to Mahanaim. By the behaviour of
the sheep God proves his ability as a Shepherd.

We have separated the different strands of thought in
these words but we have not looked at them in any depth.
We must now do this by turning to the New Testament,
looking at the leader of the sheep and seeing exactly what
he demanded from those who followed him.

The attractive leader

One of the most important dates in the Hebrew year was
the Feast of Tabernacles, which was something like our
Harvest Festival. At Tabernacle time, Jerusalem was
given a festive spirit by being crowded with more overseas
visitors than at any other time in the year. The city itself
looked quite different, with every street, square, courtyard
and roof, in fact every available space filled with the leafy
bivouacs that had given their name to the festival. Law
required that at this time of the year every Israelite should
leave his permanent dwelling and live in a tent made from
the branches of a tree. The thousands of home-made tents
that filled the city were a reminder, not only of God's past
provision in the Wilderness, but also his recent provision
in the harvest just gathered in.

The Feast of Tabernacles began on the 15th of Tishri
and it lasted for a week[1]. Tishri corresponds to our October.
The evening of the 14th of Tishri was the *illumination of the
Temple*. This particular piece of pageantry was held in the
Court of Women, the second of the Temple areas. No
Gentile was allowed inside this court and no Israelite woman
could progress nearer to the sanctuary. The whole of the
Court of Women was surrounded by a colonnade of white
marble pillars standing some 25 feet high; going into the
Court of Women by the Beautiful Gate, the colonnade on
the far side of the Court was called Solomon's Porch. This
porch housed the Temple Treasury, consisting of thirteen

chests into which the Israelite placed his temple tax offerings.

For the ceremony of Illumination and every subsequent night of the Feast of Tabernacles, four huge candelabras were lit in the Court of Women and they shone so brightly that they lit the whole city.

On the day after the Feast, Jesus was teaching in Solomon's Porch, a favourite place for the teachers to expound the law, because the Temple Treasury guaranteed an audience. Even if the four candelabras had been removed by the time that Jesus spoke, they must have been very much in the minds of the people as he said '*I am the Light of the World*'. And what an incredible claim this was. The inference was quite clear: Jesus was stating that he was a brighter light than that given out by the four candelabras. The candelabras had merely lit Jerusalem; Jesus was claiming that he would light up the whole world.

Nearly two thousand years after the event, we can see how the words of Jesus in Solomon's Porch have been fulfilled. So attractive is his leadership, that in the twentieth century he has followers on every continent. His disciples are to be found in every social class of people of every colour and language. Here is the world's most magnetic leader.

Keep out of sight

Jesus went on in Solomon's Porch to promise that those who followed him would share in this light. We must now go on to discover what it means to follow Jesus.

'Then Jesus told his disciples, "If any man would come after me, *let him deny himself*".' (Matthew 16·24).

In this passage Matthew uses the most distinctive New Testament name for the followers of Jesus: they are his *disciples*, or his *learners*. And the first thing that the disciple has to learn is that he must deny himself. Like all negative statements, at first sight this demand appears more difficult and less inviting than it actually is. If you put it round the other way you will see that Jesus is saying that God's will, rather than our own, is to be promoted in our lives. John the Baptist expressed it in the most delightful way. He said, 'he must increase, but I must decrease' (John 3·30). In the last chapter, we saw that the disciple must exchange his own perishing life for the imperishable life of God, so it is understandable that God should now be at the centre of that life.

This is difficult for a man, because the natural thing for him to do is to assert himself. The classic example of this is seen in poet's corner in Westminster Abbey where there is a plaque erected to the author of one of the great master-pieces of English literature. The stone reads:

In the Year of Our Lord Christ
One thousand seven hundred and thirty seven
This bust of the author of Paradise Lost
Was placed here by William Benson Esq.,
One of the auditors of the Imprest
To H. M. King George II
Formerly
Surveyor General of the Works
of H. M. George I.

The monument does not even mention John Milton! The majority of the words are words of self praise to Mr. William Benson.

By similar self-assertion, what monuments of prayer, respectability and work we erect so that people may see what we have done. Because we have worked purely by human endeavour, our spiritual achievements are almost nil. If we would only do as Jesus suggests, putting God in the centre of our lives, then the possibilities of spiritual success are limitless.

This is well illustrated in the life of a young man called Ian Thomas,[2] who became a christian at the age of twelve, and almost straight away felt that he should become a missionary when he left school. When he was seventeen, he went to St Bartholomew's Hospital in London to train to be a doctor in preparation for missionary work. He quickly became a leader of the Christian Union in the Hospital and soon every available moment was spent in counselling and talking to others about spiritual things, but without any success at all.

At the age of nineteen Ian Thomas felt a spiritual failure. There was little point in going abroad when he had not learned to serve God successfully at home. He knelt by his bed and wept. His Bible fell open at Philippians 1·21 where Paul says 'To me to live is Christ', and that night Jesus seemed to say to Ian Thomas, 'For seven years you have been trying to live *for* me, and for those seven years I have been wanting to live through you'. That night Ian Thomas began to learn the lesson of letting Jesus be at the centre of his life.

The first thing that a disciple has to learn, is to get out of the way, so that Jesus can be seen to be at work through him.

Single Minded

Then a follower of Jesus has to learn to be single minded in his discipleship. To teach this, Jesus used a most striking phrase. 'If any man would come after me, let him deny himself and *take up his cross*'. Jesus only had to utter these words to evoke a grim picture in the minds of his hearers. For among many unpleasant things, Roman occupation had meant the introduction of crucifixion as a form of punishment, and the Romans crucified people for the most trivial of offences. So the sight of a platoon of soldiers marching a prisoner staggering under the weight of a cross was a common affair. One of the most noticeable things about those condemned to crucifixion was that so much concentration was necessary simply to carry a cross that the prisoner had strength for little else. A man carrying a cross could walk past familiar places without even noticing that they were there. Jesus says that this is a picture of the single mindedness that his followers must show in discipleship.

Do you follow me?

Finally the disciple must learn to be completely obedient to Jesus in every sphere of his life. Jesus put it like this. 'If any man would come after me, let him deny himself and take up his cross and *follow me*'. The words 'follow me' which Jesus uses here, are words with a great variety of uses, which reveal the breadth of the appeal to obedience that Jesus is making upon his disciples. These are the words that an officer would use as he ordered his soldiers to charge, just as they are the words that a teacher would use as he began to lead his pupils through a complicated intellectual principle on a blackboard. These are the words that a master would use in an arbitrary fashion to his slave. From his disciples Jesus asks physical and intellectual obedience, no matter how arbitrary that demand appears to be.

The Church of Judas

David has spoken in this psalm of the one who leads us into paths of righteousness. We have looked at the leader; the most attractive leader that the world has yet seen. And we have also seen what it means to follow him. To know the leader and not to follow him is to betray him, because having restored us he leads us into paths of righteousness for his name's sake. Belief and behaviour are inseparably tied together. J. Hollis Walker, a Methodist minister, has written a book called *The Church of Judas*. This may sound a strange title for a book by a Christian minister, but the author tells us that he did not choose the title because he thought that Judas was utterly bad but because he thought that Judas loved Christ and yet betrayed him. Mr. Walker goes on to say that this is exactly what the church is doing in our time. The failure of Judas was not a failure of belief but of behaviour. We tie our behaviour to our belief in Jesus when we begin to live life his way.

1. *The Talmud* Frederick Warne & Co. Ltd., page 349.
2. *They found the Secret* by V. Raymond Edman, Zondermann, page 138.

'Even though I walk through
the valley of the shadow of death
I fear no evil'

Psalm 23·4

Mumps and Measles of the Soul

We have now come to the place where we must look at the *valley of the shadow of death*. Two modern shepherds have described in detail this particular valley. Ferando D'Alfonso, the Basque shepherd,[1] says that there is a valley of the shadow of death in Palestine. South of the Jericho road leading from Jerusalem to the Dead Sea, it is a continuation of the Kedron valley and becomes a narrow defile through the mountain range. It is necessary to pass through this valley from the pastures of David to those of Abraham. The valley is four and a half miles long, its walls over 1,500 feet high; in places the floor of the valley is only ten or twelve feet wide. It is not easy to travel through the valley because its floor surface has been badly eroded by cloudbursts, forming gullys seven or eight feet deep. The actual footing on solid rock is so narrow in some places that flocks of sheep cannot pass; and so there is an unwritten rule that the sheep must go up the valley in the morning and down in the evening. Another modern shepherd, Stephen Harboush, in his book *My Shepherd Life in Galilee*[2] calls this valley *the valley of fire* (wadi el-naar), which he says is five hundred feet below sea level and, apart from the area of the Dead Sea itself, is the hottest place in Palestine.

The night is long that never finds the day

Most translators refer to this valley as the *valley of the shadow of death*; yet it is almost universally accepted that the words are derived from a root that means *deep gloom*[3]. And the translators of the Revised Standard Version would seem to agree with this, because on the thirteen other occasions that the phrase occurs it is either translated as 'gloom' or 'darkness'. So the idea behind the words is not the *valley of the shadow of death*, but the *valley of deep gloom*. And this is a valley which many people have to experience today in the form of depression.

So in this chapter we are going to look at depression, that experience that Charles Lamb referred to as *mumps and measles of the soul;* something with which Winston Churchill was so familiar that he even had a nickname for it, calling it the *Black Dog*.

For depressed people, death has little meaning, because they only have to die once; but they have to get up and live three hundred and sixty-five times a year. So for them *the night is long that never finds the day.* It is inevitable that some Christian people will be depressed or go through other forms of mental breakdown. To suggest otherwise, says Francis Schaeffer, is a 'kind of murder', because it brings unnecessary feelings of guilt.

If only it were toothache

Those who live in the day and never experience the long night of depression normally fail to appreciate the excruciating pain of this illness. Ruth Fowke writes about someone who became depressed because of taking drugs prescribed to prevent blindness. In the end he preferred the prospect of total blindness rather than the depression caused by the drugs. If the pain of depression is misunderstood, then the illness is more so. Florence Nightingale said

'Oh, if one has but a toothache what remedies are invented, what carriages, horses, ponies, journeys, doctors, chaperones, are urged upon us, but if it is something to do with the mind, unless it belongs to one of the three heads – loss of friends, loss of fortune, or loss of health – it is neither believed nor understood, and every different kind of suffering is ranged under the comprehensive heading "fancy", and disposed of in one comprehensive remedy, concealment or self-communion, which is the same thing.'[4]

The eighteenth century poet and hymn writer, William Cowper, friend of John Newton, suffered periods of acute depression; he said that other illnesses only battered the walls of the mind but depression crept silently into the citadel and put the garrison to sword.

Unspeakable gloom

There is no one symptom of depression: it comes in a variety of forms. James Mossman, whom Robin Day described as one of 'the most brilliant of reporters who helped to build up television journalism when it started in the nineteen fifties' had 'attacks of unspeakable gloom'.[5] Another form of depression is despair. Lord Willis, one of the five sons of a London bus driver, who created such television successes as *Mrs Thursday*, *Dixon of Dock Green* and *Sergeant Cork* says 'my friends wouldn't regard me as an introspective man, but I am, in many ways. I have this outward-going manner and appearance, and I can assume it like a mask. But I have these extraordinary days of despair – not for myself or for my own writing, although sometimes for that – but for the world.'[6]

The causes of depression

The first causes of depression are quite natural. Depression is the natural reaction of the mind to upheavals within the body. To some degree, we must expect some form of depression at puberty, childbirth, illness, menstruation and menopause. Dr John Hercus says 'the tangled emotional wires in the working of the female may make her more likely to be the moody member' of the human race.

Then, of course, depression is the natural reaction to upheavals outside the body, such as disappointment, sorrow, grief. These upheavals outside the body wound the mind; but they are all, in the first place, clean wounds and, given time, will heal. Depression is part of that healing process beginning to work.

Patho-phobic, hypochondriacal, narcissistic self

There are some people who are born with temperamental weaknesses that make them inclined towards depression. In June 1803 Victor Hugo, aged sixteen months, was found in a corner weeping silently for no apparent reason. His biographer, Andre Maurois, says 'thus it was that a melancholic strain developed in his character, a strain which overcame his prodigious vitality from time to time throughout his life'. Many Christian people experience a similar temperamental weakness to depression. Catherine Booth, wife of the founder of the Salvation Army, says 'darkness gathers thicker than ever around the path I tread, and doubt, gloom, melancholy and despair'. The famous preacher, R. W. Dale of Birmingham, wrote 'seasons of depression, heavy, terrible, overwhelming come over me without apparently any definite cause, and stay in spite of means which seem most powerful to effect their removal.' Raynor C. Johnson in his book *The Light and the Gate* speaks of his intimate friendship and correspondence with the Methodist minister Dr Leslie Weatherhead. We are told how, in February 1957, Dr Weatherhead went to the West Indies with friends in an attempt to cure his depression and insomnia; but how, on his return to London, the old symptoms immediately returned, and he went through many months of dark depression. In May of that year for the first time he mentioned his retirement, and he spoke of himself as 'a patho-phobic, hypochondriacal, narcissistic old–'.[7]

Careless living

Quite clearly, depression can result from natural and temperamental causes, but a great deal of depression has a
spiritual origin. Edward Wilson, who died in the ill-fated
Antarctic expedition of 1912, wrote *look at life carelessly*;
but you cannot be without care when the words 'if only'
continually spring to mind – as they must have done for
David at Mahanaim. If only he hadn't married a foreigner;
if only he had been a better father to Absalom; if only he
had not drifted away from God over the past few years; if
only . . . To be careless, the guilt of the past must be dealt
with. Emil Brunner, in his book *The Mediator* says 'we cannot
live without God, but also we cannot live with God so long
as our guilt is not expiated. We cannot simply become
good friends once more. The wrath of God is not a mood:
it is an actual force.'[8]

Depression will certainly arise in our lives if we have not
experienced God's forgiveness – just as it will if we are not
forgiving about the actions of others in the past. Emmanuel
Kant, the philosopher, had a manservant called Lampe who
systematically embezzled money from his master over the
years. This was discovered by Kant, and Lampe was dis-
missed. 'I forgive you,' said the great philosopher, 'go'.
But it was never real forgiveness, for day after day the philosopher's diary begins with the words 'remember to forget
Lampe'.

All them supposes

There was a miserable Christian lady who always envied the
cheerfulness of her housekeeper Nancy.

'It's all very well for you, Nancy,' she used to say, 'but
you never really stop to think about the future. Suppose
you were taken ill, for instance. Suppose you were unable
to work.'

'Stop!' said Nancy. 'I never "suppose". The Lord is

my Shepherd and I know that I shall not want,' she added, to her gloomy employer. 'It's all them "*supposes*" that are making you miserable. You'd better give them all up and just trust in the Lord.'

Habakkuk sums this up in chapter 3, verse 17:

> 'Though the fig tree do not blossom
> nor the fruit be on the vines,
> the produce of the olive fail
> and the fields yield no food,
> the flock be cut off from the fold . . .'

There never has been a day when there has been absolutely no blossom on the fig trees, or vines have been completely without fruit and the yield of the fields has been nil; nor has there ever been a day when the flock was completely cut off from the fold. Depression can easily creep into our lives, when we do not allow God to deal with the past. Equally, depression will come into our lives when we do not leave the future in God's hands, when we do not learn to live in what Sir William Osler, former Regius Professor of Medicine at Oxford, once called '*daytight compartments*'. Robert Louis Stevenson said 'Anyone can carry his burdens, however hard, until nightfall. Anyone can do his work, however hard, for one day. Anyone can live sweetly, patiently, lovingly, purely until the sun goes down; and this is what life means.' It is about time we gave up all '*them supposes*' and learned to live life a day at a time.

Enjoying the lemonade

For life to be enjoyable it is not merely a matter of being careless of the past, or even dropping a few of the 'supposes' about the future. It is sometimes just a question of the present. Depression can come when life becomes a bore. Life becomes boring when we commit the sin that the church in the past called 'sloth'. Ian Fleming, the creator of James Bond, writes about it as 'sloth, that awful boredom which would engulf whole towns in the middle ages and which, because it was a denial of life itself, is an offence against God and the church'. It was this boredom, this denial of life, that was the source of Ian Fleming's own black melancholy; and it was boredom that finally destroyed his relationships with women. In a passage which is quite clearly autobiographical, Ian Fleming unsentimentally describes the process through the character of James Bond:

'With most women his manner was a mixture of taciturnity and passion. The lengthy approaches to a seduction bored him almost as much as the subsequent mess of disen- tanglement. He found something grisly in the inevitability of the pattern of each affair. The conventional parabola – sentiment, the touch of the hand, the kiss, the passionate kiss, the feel of the body, bed, then more bed, then less bed, then the boredom, the tears, and the final bitterness – was to him shameful and hypocritical.'[9]

Now if you translate that inevitable pattern of sloth to other areas of a man's life – for example, his business life – you will also see depression appearing, and the parabola will then be: 'in a job, more job, less job, then boredom'.

For the Christian to be without depression there must be a real living for God *today*. We must not be the sort of Christian that George Target speaks about when he says:

'They don't smoke, but neither do they breathe fresh air very deeply.

They don't drink wine, but neither do they enjoy lemon- ade; they don't swear, but neither do they glory in any magnificent words, neither poetry nor prayer:

they don't gamble, but neither do they take much chance on God;

they don't look at women and girls with lust in their hearts, but neither do they roll breathless with love and laughter, naked under the sun of high summer.

It's all rather pale and round-shouldered, the great Prince in prison lying.'[10]

This is the day

The psychologists tell us that we react in one of four ways to every problem that confronts us. We either *flee* it, *fight* it, *forget* it, or *face* it. We quite clearly cannot *fight* depression. Men have tried to, and they have failed. We cannot *flee* it; if we are experiencing depression, it surrounds us at all times. We cannot *forget* it, for the very same reason: it is always there. Therefore we have to *face* it. And it is that resolution that can turn the weakness into something that builds our character. Anthony Storr wrote in a study of Winston Churchill in the *Observer* for March 30th 1969, called 'The Enemy Within':

> 'Churchill, in spite of his aristocratic birth and social position, started life with disadvantages which he never wholly conquered; although his whole career was an effort to overcome them. Without these disadvantages he would have been a happier, more ordinary, better-balanced and lesser human being. But had he been a stable and equable man he could never have inspired the nation... For Winston Churchill suffered from prolonged and recurrent fits of depression; and no understanding of his character is possible unless this central fact is taken into account. His own name for depression was "Black Dog": and the fact that he had a nickname for it argues that it was all too familiar a companion . . . The more one examines Winston Churchill as a person, the more one is forced to the conclusion that his aggressiveness, his courage and his dominance were not rooted in his inheritance, but were the product of deliberate decision and iron will.'[11]

F. W. Boreham describes how he visited a Sussex village to take the anniversary services at a little chapel. He arrived late on the Saturday evening and was taken to a little ivy covered cottage, owned by Bessie, the widow of a former minister. F. W. Boreham went straight to bed and slept soundly, only to be awoken by the strong sunlight of a June morning. He sprang out of bed to draw the curtains and catch the first glimpse of the village in which he was to preach.

Across the glass of the window were the words THIS IS THE DAY. They had been cut into the glass with a stone. He asked Bessie about it at breakfast.

'Oh, everybody asks about that,' she said with a laugh, as soon as the subject was broached.

'I never thought when I wrote it there that it would lead to so many questions. But you see, I've had a lot of trouble in my life, and I'm a great one for worrying, always afraid of what's going to happen tomorrow, and each morning when I woke up I felt that the whole weight of the world was upon me.

'One day, when I was very upset about things, I was reading my Bible and I came across these words in the twenty-fourth verse of Psalm 118: "This is the day which the Lord has made; let us rejoice and be glad in it".'

Old Bessie went on to say that she wondered which day was referred to in particular. Then it occurred to her that it meant any day, every day, today. She printed those words on her bedroom window so that, as soon as she drew the curtains, no matter what sort of day lay beyond she would know that before it was written the reminder: 'This is the day which the Lord has made'.[12]

That is exactly what we find Habakkuk saying in verse 18 of chapter 3. He says that whatever sort of day it is going to be, he will rejoice in the Lord, he will joy in the God of his salvation. We cannot change the day, but we can change our attitude by the way we face that day, by the reminder that it is the day that God has chosen for us. Each day that Old Bessie drew her curtains would be different: some would be stormy and some would be sunny. Depression is as inconsistent as the weather; but depression, like the storm, will not last for ever.

Getting a new seat in the saddle

1964 was a bad year for Dale Evans and her cowboy husband Roy Rogers. Roy Rogers had to spend a good deal of time in hospital after an operation, and their twelve-year-old adopted daughter Debbie was killed in a road accident on the San Diego freeway. Dale Evans described how her Christian friends helped her, and says in her biography, 'I slowly gained control and got a new seat in the saddle.' Getting astride life again can be a slow process. Bishop Ryle said 'The spirit of darkness comes on horseback and goes on foot'.

But God is going to help us. Habukkuk goes on in chapter three to say 'God, the Lord, is my strength, he makes my feet like hinds' feet, he makes me tread up on *my* high places.' We are not promised that one day we will walk on God's high places; we are not even promised that we will walk on the high places enjoyed by other Christians. But the emphatic promise here is that we will walk on our own high places. In other words, we will come out of the valley of deep gloom.

In this verse the depressed person is promised all that is necessary to come out of the gloomy valley. One of the worst feelings in depression is that you will not be able to last the course. You will not be strong enough to face it; so in the first line of the verse we are promised *spiritual strength*. While we are experiencing depression we may be conscious of the weakness of our own body. We feel, perhaps, that we may stumble as we walk up or down steps. But in the second line we are promised *spiritual stability*: 'He will make my feet like hinds' feet'. Finally, we are promised *spiritual serenity*: 'He makes me tread upon my high places'. It is not God's plan that we should spend all our time in the gloomy valley. Francis de Sale said 'The evil one is pleased with sadness and melancholy'. God's plan is to lift us out of the gloomy valley *to the spiritual Wadi Fara.*

1. Article from *National Wool Growers' Association* leaflet (USA) by James K. Wallace
2. *My Shepherd Life in Galilee* by Stephen Harboush, Harper & Row, page 39
3. *Cambridge Bible, Psalms vol 1* by A. F. Kirkpatrick, Cambridge University Press, page 126.
4. *Florence Nightingale and the Doctors* by Sir Zachary Cope, Museum Press.
5. Article from the *Evening Standard*, April 6th 1971
6. Article from the *TV Times*, April 9th 1970.
7. *The Light and the Gate* by Raynor C. Johnson, Hodder & Stoughton, page 277.
8. *The Mediator* by Emil Brunner, Lutterworth, page 482.
9. *The Life of Ian Fleming* by John Pearson, Jonathan Cape, page 86.
10. *Contact*, February 1969.
11. Article from *The Observer*, March 30th 1969, by Anthony Storr.
12. *Shadows on the Wall* by F.W. Boreham, Epworth Press, page 74.

'For thou art with me;
thy rod and thy staff,
they comfort me.'
                    Psalm 23·4

The Treasures of the Darkness

Lord Wolseley, one of the most distinguished soldiers of the last century, wrote a slender volume in 1872 entitled *The Soldiers' Pocketbook*. In it he said:

> 'In all siege operations, it is most important that the staff and the Royal Engineer officers should study the almanack well and keep before them the hours of sunset and sunrise, so that all possible advantage be reaped of every hour of darkness.'

That last phrase, with its encouragement to take every advantage of the darkness, has always intrigued me. I think we often react so violently against suffering that we fail to discover either its purpose or its benefits. Isaiah speaks of 'the treasures of darkness' (Isaiah 45.3); and it is these that we are going to try to discover in this chapter.

Where eagles dare

I began to glimpse the purpose of suffering and adversity from the fact that Moses, after forty years in the wilderness, did not complain about the experience but *sang* that God had been working 'like an eagle that stirs up its nest' (Deuteronomy 32·11). To this day, that is precisely how an eagle teaches its young to fly. It makes a nest in a high and inaccessible mountain eyrie from sparse and prickly twigs collected from the mountainside; but to protect the eggs and the baby eagles the nest is lined with soft animal fur and thistledown. With such a comfortable home, and with a long drop to the outside world, there is not very much incentive for baby eagles to begin flying, so at the appropriate moment the parent eagle 'stirs up its nest'. The soft fur and down is removed and the sharp branches force the baby eagle to stand on the very edge of the nest. In the end tiredness makes it fall out; but as Moses noticed the falling eagle is accompanied by a falling parent that 'flutters over its young, spreading out its wings, catching them, bearing them on its pinions'. The parent falls with the baby in case it does not learn to fly. When it does, the parent soon moves away, leaving the young eagle to soar high above the sharp prodding branches which had thrust it from the comfortable security of the nest. Where eagles dare, they learn to fly. So often the sufferings and adversities of life are the proddings of God. If only we would dare to take the plunge, maybe we would find that we could use our spiritual wings.

All sunshine makes a desert

It is often quite remarkable how productive suffering is. Marine scientists tell us that pearls are produced by pain. A tiny parasitic worm bores through the shell of the oyster, and the movement of water eventually carries a speck of sand into the now unprotected, sensitive body inside. To stop the irritation the oyster excretes a substance to cover the irritant; but the irritation is never wholly removed by being covered up, so the process of stopping it continues and a pearl comes into being.

In his Braemar home in 1881, Lloyd Osborne, the twelve-year-old stepson of a young Scottish barrister, lay seriously ill. One day, while visiting the boy, his father drew a strange-looking island on a piece of paper which he afterwards said looked like 'a fat dragon standing up'. For amusement the boy and his father – whose name was Robert Louis Stevenson – added landmarks to the island, nonsense-sounding names such as Spyglass Hill and Foremast Hill; and so the germ of *Treasure Island* came into being. The following morning Stevenson wrote the first chapter of the book, resolving to add a chapter every morning in order to have something to read to his stepson in the afternoon. The afternoon readings began as a quiet affair, but soon the whole household and, later on, visitors were gathering for the next instalment. From that sick room came a masterpiece read by millions all over the world.

We often long for the trouble-free life, just to lie in the sun and to do nothing. But when we do that we forget the logic of the old Arabian proverb that *all sunshine makes a desert*.

Christianity does not abolish suffering

When J. Sidlow Baxter got married, his mother said to him 'Well now, you've come to the end of your troubles – *this* end'. Christianity without suffering is not the Christianity of the New Testament. Not once did Jesus show his followers how to escape life; rather, he showed them how to live life with his help, no matter how difficult they found it. And Christianity today does not promise to give us a bypass to life so that we may escape the problems of living; Christianity often leads us straight into suffering. John Stott says 'many Christian writers have recognised in more recent days that suffering is the hallmark of the genuine church'[1]. Certainly, one of the marks of the true believer is that he rejoices 'in suffering'. That phrase is put in a much stronger way in the Authorised Version, which translates it 'we glory in tribulation' (Romans 5.3). Our word *tribulation* comes from the Latin word *tribulum* which was a Roman threshing instrument: a heavy wooden platform, several inches thick, about the size of a large dining table. The underneath of this platform was studded with flints and nails and the ox would drag the tribulum backwards and forwards across the harvested corn, dividing the wheat from the chaff.

If suffering is the hallmark of the genuine church, it is also quite clearly the experience of every true believer. We can rejoice in sufferings, because we know that by them God is dividing the wheat from the chaff.

Sweet are the uses of adversity

So far, we have established one or two truths about the treasure of the darkness, but we have not really looked at the treasure itself. As we turn now to look more specifically at the second half of verse 4, we find that David says that adversity has its uses. The valley of deep gloom, whether it comes to us in the form of physical, mental or spiritual suffering, can make us aware of the reality of the Shepherd's presence, just as it can enable us to enjoy the comfort of the Shepherd's equipment.

A significant change takes place in verse 4 of Psalm 23. You will see it straight away if you notice that the pronouns change from 'he' to 'thou'. In other words, up to this point in the psalm David had been talking about God; but now, for the first time, he starts to talk directly to him. Again, it is helpful to notice that it is not on the top of a spiritual mountain but in a valley that David has this intimate experience of God.

Closer than breathing

In verse 4 David very simply says 'thou art with me.' It is difficult to reproduce the emphatic way that the Bible speaks about the presence of God. Tennyson came somewhere near to it when he said, 'closer is he than breathing and nearer than hands or feet'. Often the strongest statements about God's presence are hidden in the original language and do not appear in our translations.

In English, two negatives simply cancel each other out. But in Greek, the more negatives there are, the more emphatic and categorical the statement. One place where negatives are used to emphasise God's nearness is Hebrews 13.5, which reads in our translation 'I will never fail you nor forsake you.' In the Greek, five of the words there are negatives, so the only way you can give the phrase its full force is to translate it like this: 'I will *never* leave you *nor* forsake you, *not never no-how*.' Or, if you prefer it, 'I will never, never fail you; I will never, never, never forsake you'.

John McNeill began life working as a porter for the old London Midland and Scottish Railway. At first he worked in his home village of Inverkip, but the day came when he was promoted to the larger station of Greenock. So that he could be with his parents on Sunday he had to walk the seven miles from Greenock very late on Saturday night. For two of the miles outside Inverkip the road was particularly black, with high wooded hills on both sides. John McNeill's feet hardly touched the ground as he ran along that dark piece of the road. One night, when a storm made the road even darker, and his heart was pounding, he suddenly heard a voice. The voice said 'Is that you, John?' It was his father who had come to meet him. This experience John McNeill frequently used to illustrate that the Father, the Shepherd God, meets us at the very depth of the gloomy valley. He has promised never to fail us, or forsake us, not, never, no-how.

The Shepherd's equipment

Of course we cannot be certain what David was wearing in the hill country of Mahanaim after he had escaped with his soldiers and family, but we can be fairly certain what he used to wear as a shepherd boy when out in the hills of Judea. He would have had some sort of head covering: a primitive form of sun-hat, a piece of material held in place by a length of camel's hair rope about half an inch thick. He would wear a coarse shirt, gathered at the waist with a rough leather belt; over this at night and in cold weather would be a warm sleeveless woollen garment. Apart from his clothes the shepherd would have four pieces of equipment. Only two of these are mentioned in this verse, but we will look at all four.

The shepherd's staff. With his staff or crook the shepherd would catch sheep which were going astray; he would also use it at night when the sheep were entering the fold. As he held it close to the ground, the sheep were forced under it, enabling the shepherd to examine them individually for injuries.

We are often forced low by God so that the injuries of life can be dealt with quickly before they develop into something much more serious. Spiritually, to be under God's staff can be a pretty humbling experience, especially if one has been a Christian for a number of years. We may find that we lose our assurance, or the death of a friend may bring back the chilling fear of the grave. To see other Christians going through the same experience can also affect our lives: the financial or moral failure of someone within our church can make us sceptical about God's ability to keep and protect. And, on a larger scale, we may become depressed and frightened by the state of the world today.

It has taken me a long time to learn, but after eighteen years as a Christian I am beginning to be thankful when I am hardpressed by the Shepherd. If I am honest, when he brings me low it is because he has a finger on a bruise; and when I examine my life at such a moment there are nearly always things that need to be confessed, or great doctrines that need to be rediscovered and re-experienced. I personally am glad that I have a Shepherd God who is so concerned that he forces me low with his crook to make me aware of my own needs and to allow him to heal me.

The Shepherd's rod. This was a short club about two feet long, with a heavy bitumen head. Into the head had been fixed pieces of flint and metal. At the handle end was a leather loop that would be put over the shepherd's wrist so that it would not be lost when he was using it to protect the flock from wild animals. I suppose that, if the sheep had been able to absorb and reflect on all that happened around them each day, they would have been amazed that the shepherd, who was so kind and patient with them, seemed so violent and destructive with marauding animals; that the shepherd, who used his staff to see that they stayed with the flock and were fit and well, would use his rod to destroy the bears and snakes that might endanger their lives.

There is encouragement here. God's people may be harrassed by evil in a particular age. They may even decline because of the forces of evil arrayed against them. But the eternal security of the flock is guaranteed, for the Shepherd has his rod in his hand. The Shepherd shows loving kindness towards his people. He is even patient with those who wander away from him. But his rod is already raised for the destruction of all that is evil.

The shepherd's sling. The story of David and Goliath has made us imagine that David was the only person who could use a sling with any accuracy. But the sling was, in fact, a standard piece of equipment for the people of David's time, and with it literally hundreds of people reached a remarkable proficiency. There is a reference to seven hundred men of Benjamin who, with their slings, were so accurate they could hit a human hair (Judges 20·16).

The sling was not only used by the shepherd to attack and to protect. It was also used in the way that a modern shepherd would use his sheepdog. If a sheep was going astray then the shepherd would sling a shot just in front of it to turn it, bringing it back to the flock. I think the great Shepherd still does this in a spiritual sense. As we go astray, he has ways of turning us to bring us back. I once remember saying at a meeting that I thought there were two things necessary for spiritual failure; the first was *temptation*, but this had to coincide with the second, *opportunity*. I went on to say that God often stops his people failing by not allowing both these things to happen at once. If you like, with a spiritual sling-shot he knocks either the opportunity or the temptation

77

aside. Not long after that meeting I received a letter from a young City man which said:

> 'What you had to say today about God preventing temptation and opportunity coinciding has been so true in my life. I've been a Christian for about three years, and very happily married for the past year. We both became Christians together, but six months before our marriage we had a week of disagreement, which ended with a terrific row on the Friday lunchtime. We decided to finish with each other. That afternoon I asked a very pretty girl in the office to come away with me for the weekend, and we went to a peaceful country hotel. We had a quiet dinner and went up to our room. The opportunity was there, but the temptation simply went. I believe that the Shepherd just hit it out of the way with an accurately placed slingshot. We sat up all night talking and then drove back to London early the next day. I really believe that God protected me that night from something that would have harmed my spiritual life and future marriage.'

The shepherd's scrip. This was that leather pouch that hung from a man's belt. The shepherd would carry in his scrip some parched grain, dried fruit, olives and cheese. The provision would be largely for himself, but there would be titbits for the sheep during the day.

Often we imagine that God's provision only extends to the great things in life, and forget that the Shepherd carries a scrip in his belt. There are tiny morsels of provision and encouragement for every moment of the day.

When the worst comes to the worst

There is an interesting phrase in Peter's first letter where he refers to those 'who by God's power are guarded through faith for salvation ready to be revealed *in the last time* (1 Peter 1·5). Those last four words can be translated 'when the worst comes to the worst'. That is what David is saying here in verse 4: 'even though I walk through the valley of the shadow of death, I fear no evil; for thou art with me; thy rod and thy staff, they *comfort* me'. The root of the word *comfort* is *repent*; and, in fact, that is the way this Hebrew word is more often translated. After much suffering Job says 'I know that thou canst do all things . . . I had heard of thee by the hearing of the ear, but now my eye sees thee, therefore I despise myself and *repent* in dust and ashes (Job 42·2,5,6). What Job is clearly saying here is that previously he had heard God was mighty; but now he had experienced God to be all-powerful, and that experience had moved him to repentance. Repentance was a comforting experience for Job because through it he had discovered just how strong God was.

So, if *the worst comes to the worst*, if we are asked to go through a terrible valley experience, either physical, mental or spiritual, we are going to progress from the place where we had merely heard with our ears to a place where we can experience the mighty presence and equipment of the Shepherd. These are the treasures of the darkness.

1. *What Christ Thinks of the Church*, by J. R. W. Stott, Lutterworth Press, page 42.

'Thou preparest a table before me
in the presence of my enemies;
thou anointest my head with oil,
my cup overflows'

Psalm 23·5

The Badge of Victory

The majority of commentators on this psalm say that the pastoral image of the shepherd ends with verse four, and that in the last two verses we have the picture of a fugitive in an eastern court. In verse five we see the splendour of an eastern banquet where the guests were anointed with sweet-scented spikenard and where the hospitality was so lavish that cups overflowed with wine. Eastern etiquette meant that to enjoy hospitality was also to enjoy sanctuary: So in these words we see the fugitive refreshing himself, while his enemies are forced to stand by unable to raise a hand to do him harm. One writer goes as far as saying that David had exhausted the metaphor of a shepherd and had to find a new one so that he could give the psalm a happy ending!

Now it seems to me that the beauty of one of the most perfect pieces of literature, as well as of spiritual writing, is immediately destroyed if you say that the first four verses have nothing to do with the last two. So it is without any hesitation that I say that the six verses of the psalm form a unity, and therefore the pastoral image of a shepherd and his sheep goes right to the end of verse six.

The badge of victory

In the last chapter I mentioned that John McNeill began his life as a porter at Inverkip Station in Scotland. This Station was served by the old London Midland and Scottish Railway, which was always known by the initials LMS, so that the badge that John McNeill wore on his cap as a porter simply said 'LMS'.

John McNeill left the railway company in his early twenties to go to theological college in Edinburgh to train to be a minister. Even when he became a famous evangelist who travelled the world, he always kept his old cap badge in his pocket, telling anyone who inquired that LMS stood for the *Lord* is *My Shepherd*. Quite clearly, for John McNeill to have LMS on his cap was to have the emblem of safety and the badge of victory.

Emblems of Safety

Unlike the biblical commentators, two modern authors Faduel Moghahghab[1] and Ferando d'Alfonso[2] state emphatically from years of practical experience as shepherds that the picture of a shepherd must go right to the end of the psalm.

Both authors say that in the middle of the day the shepherd cleared the ground of anything that would endanger the sheep before he settled down for his midday meal and a quiet siesta. The shepherd knew that the two most dangerous enemies of the sheep were poisonous grass and snakes; so before taking his meal he would use the end of his staff to root out the poisonous grasses, putting them on large rocks to dry in the sun, so that they would die and be unable to take root again. Faduel Moghahghab writes of a cousin who lost three hundred sheep through their eating poisonous grass. The shepherd would also clear the ground of snakes, leaving the dead carcasses on rocks, but this time as a sign to other predators that the area was unsafe for them. By far the most dangerous snake was the horned viper, normally a mere eighteen inches long, which would lie in a hole in the pasture biting at the sheep as they grazed. But cobras were not unknown. One morning in 1934 Dr Leslie Weatherhead reports that he saw two large cobras within a few miles of each other in northern Palestine.[3]

No wonder the sheep felt secure as the shepherd rooted out these dangers. They refreshed themselves in the presence of their defeated enemies.

Set in battle array

The word translated *prepare* in this verse is frequently used in the Old Testament in a logistic military sense. It is used to describe men fully equipped and ready for battle; '*set in battle array*' (1 Samuel 17·2, *literally*) is another way that this same word is translated. These words bring the assurance that we can be equipped with everything that is necessary for life. Paul makes a similar promise in the New Testament when he says, 'My God will supply every need of yours according to his riches in glory in Christ Jesus' (Philippians 4·19).

'Thou preparest *a table*' is really David's way of saying that God's provision is not only abundant but is also immensely practical and everyday in its nature. That this provision is *in the face of our enemies* is something that we need to underline in the twentieth century because we seem to have left the devil out of all our spiritual thinking. Theo Preiss says, 'Since the 18th century we have reduced the religious drama to two partners, God and Man. With a superior smile we have eliminated the roles of Satan and his acolytes.'[4] To eliminate him from our thinking makes him the more dangerous because it means that we are quite unprepared for his attacks.

His satanic majesty

We have already looked at the enemies of the flock. If you had asked me a year ago to list the things that endangered the lives of sheep in the hills of Palestine, I think that I would have jotted down things like the rough ground of places like the wadi el-naar, and the marauding bears and lions that David mentions in some of the other psalms; but in a hundred years I do not think that I would have put either poisonous grasses or snakes on my list.

In a similar way it seems true that, while we are vaguely aware that the human race has a spiritual enemy, we never really stop to define exactly who he is. I think that even the euphemisms that we use for the devil blunt our perception of his reality and the deadly nature of his work. John Brown of Haddington's phrase *His Satanic Majesty*, makes him almost as amusing as the musical hall figure with horns and tail. Even C. S. Lewis's *Our Father Below* makes him as benign as Billy Bray's *Old Smutty Face*. So let us look at the devil and see the exact way that the Bible defines both his character and his work.

Know your enemy

It is important that we examine our enemy, because this is the secret of overcoming him. In the second world war the victory that Field-Marshal Lord Montgomery gained over Rommel was largely due to his painstaking study of his enemy. The Field-Marshal studied Rommel's character, his temperament, his habits and the tactics that he used in his previous battles. This enabled Lord Montgomery so to plan his campaign that he could take every advantage of Rommel's weaknesses.

What's in a name?

The answer to that is plenty, when the name is found in the Bible. For Bible names, with very few exceptions, are exact descriptions of the person who bears them. Nowhere is this more true than with the devil. In the Bible there is no attempt to glamourise him in any way. Look at some of the things he is called. He is *Satan*, meaning the Adversary. He is the *Devil*, the slanderer, the destroyer, *Be-elzebub*, the Lord of the flies. He is *Belial*, the low, the abject one; *the Wicked One, the God of this World, the Prince of Darkness, the*

Dragon, *the Tormentor, the Accuser, the Deceiver, the Liar, the Murderer, him who has the power of death, Abaddon, the Enemy, the Ruler of this World, the Tempter.* There is certainly nothing faintly amusing or benign about such names or the actions that they describe.

That hideous fall

The devil was once described as the *'Day Star'* and the *'son of Dawn'* (Isaiah 14·12). He was among the highest rank of God's angels. Ezekiel calls him a *cherub* (Ezekiel 28·14). The name of this special rank of angels possibly came from the word *to till* or *to plough*,[1] and speaks of their constant activity in the service of God. What Martin Luther called 'that hideous fall from heaven to hell' took place because of pride (Isaiah 14·13, 1 Timothy 3·6). We do not know exactly when, but obviously it was in eternity prior to time. Whenever it was, he who was among the greatest of God's angels fell to become *the Wicked One, the enemy of God* and *the deceiver* of God's people.

Majesty in ruins

The ultimate downfall of the devil is certain, because one of the reasons why Jesus came to this earth was to destroy him (Hebrews 2·14, 1 John 3·8). Nonetheless, we are foolish if we underestimate his present ability. The fact that he is a *fallen* angel refers to his wickedness and in no way suggests that he has lost spiritual power, or is less likely to attack us today. In fact he is constantly on the move against us. We are harassed by him in physical opposition; intellectually he endeavours to undermine our belief; morally he tries to erode our standards and behaviour. It is difficult to better Henry Law's description of his ceaseless activity against us:

'He never slumbers, never is weary, never relents, never abandons hope. He deals his blows alike at childhood's weakness, youth's inexperience, manhood's strength and the totterings of age. He watches to ensnare the morning thought. He departs not with the shades of night. By his legions he is everywhere, at all times. He enters the palace, the hut, the fortress, the camp, the fleet. He invades every chamber of every dwelling, every pew of every sanctuary. He is busy with the busy. He hurries about with the active. He sits by each bed of sickness and whispers into each dying ear. As the spirit quits the tenement of clay, he still draws his bow with unrelenting rage.'[6]

His defeat may be certain but he is still a real enemy: so real that some people are quite convinced that they have actually seen him. Richard Wurmbrand, the Lutheran Minister imprisoned by the Communists for fourteen years, wrote in prison, 'It is no myth that Martin Luther and many other more ordinary men have seen the devil. I saw him once as a child. He grinned at me. This is the first time I have spoken of it in a half a century. Alone in the cell, now, I felt his presence again. It was dark and cold, and he was mocking me.'[7]

Not a dead devil, but a living God

The hero's friend in Charles Reade's novel *The Cloister and the Hearth* tries to cheer him up by occasionally saying, '*Courage, comrade, the devil is dead*'. As we have seen this is not true. While his ultimate defeat may be certain he is not dead yet. In any case this is not where Christian victory lies. Our hope is not in a dead devil but in a living God. Our hope is in a God who is so powerful that he is able to prepare a banquet of victory for us in the presence of our enemy, no matter how strong that enemy may appear to be in trying to bring about our defeat. Our natural inclination towards cowardice makes us wish for a victory without actually confronting the devil, but this cannot be so. True victory is to be found in front of the devil. It is at the place of temptation that God gives us victory.

We cannot achieve our own victory. That would be to expect the sheep to root out the snakes and poisonous grasses themselves. It is the shepherd who gives victory. Although the devil is dangerous, when compared with God he is relatively insignificant. The devil is as insignificant as horned vipers and poisonous grasses are to a shepherd; although they are dangerous the shepherd is well able to deal with them.

There is a balm in Gilead

We noticed in the last chapter that at night the shepherd would individually inspect his sheep for cuts and bruises as they entered the narrow door of the sheep fold. If he discovered injuries he would rub in a little oil to aid healing. '*Thou anointest my head with oil*', says David. In spite of a powerful God it is easy to lose our sense of victory, not necessarily from the major thrusts of the evil one, but more often from the spiritual scratches and bruises of everyday living. Emotional grazes, bruised consciences have to be healed just as much as minds that have been pummelled with the lies and deceits of the prince of darkness. Nightly we can have the healing oils of forgiveness. There is still a balm in Gilead.

There is also refreshment, for David says that his '*cup overflows*'. For some reason sheep will not drink from half-empty containers, so the shepherd had to make sure that they overflowed with water. And our refreshment is clearly of the overflowing kind too. Jesus said: '*If any one thirst, let him come to me and drink . . . and out of his heart shall flow rivers of living water*' (John 7·37).

1. *The Song of our Syrian Guest* by W. A. Knight, Stirling Tract Enterprise, page 11.
2. Article from *National Wool Grower's Association* (USA) leaflet, by James K. Wallace.
3. *A Shepherd Remembers* by Leslie Weatherhead, Hodder and Stoughton, page 159.
4. *Life of Christ* by Theo Preiss, S.C.M.
5. *The Unseen Army* by Herbert Lockyer, Upperton Press, page 25.
6. *The Gospel in Genesis* by Henry Law.
7. *In God's Underground* by Richard Wurmbrand, W. H. Allen, page 65.

'Surely goodness and mercy shall follow me
all the days of my life;
and I shall dwell in the house of the Lord
for ever.'

Psalm 23·6.

The Hounds of Heaven

Dr George Adam Smith, the Old Testament scholar who lived at the beginning of the century, had an intriguing translation for the first part of verse 6. He put it like this 'Surely goodness and mercy will follow me *or hunt me*, all the days of my life.'[1] He is saying that in this verse we see a picture of the dogs that brought up the rear of the flock. This translation seems to be fair since one marginal reading allows that goodness and mercy shall pursue us *dogging* our footsteps.[2]

In chapter 7, when we were looking at the shepherd's equipment, we saw that the shepherd of Bible times used his sling in the same way that a modern shepherd would use a dog to keep the sheep in order; but I was careful not to suggest in that chapter that the biblical shepherds were completely without dogs. They certainly did have dogs – and used them to hunt out the stragglers to bring them back to the flock. W. M. Thompson in *The Land of the Book* says that the shepherd walked before the sheep, and they followed after, while the dogs brought up the rear.[3] So the picture that we have in this verse is of a goodness and mercy that doggedly pursues us, to hunt us out.

It was this thought behind verse 6 that gave Francis Thompson the idea for his poem *The Hound of Heaven*; and it was this poem that brought Dale Evans, the wife of the film star cowboy Roy Rogers, back to God. When she read the poem she said:

'I saw that it told my own story of running and hiding from God, over eighteen years, of sunshine and shadow, toil and pleasure, success and defeat, trying hard to get out of my life the sound of those steady strong, haunting feet that followed me everywhere.'[4]

Hunted by the hounds

David says, '*Surely* goodness and mercy will hunt after me'. In David's mind there is no doubt about it. For him God's pursuit was as relentless as it was in the experience of Dale Evans and in the poem of Francis Thompson.

The word *goodness* here is often translated *pleasant*, or *enjoyable* or even *agreeable*. So it is a very striking thing that David can say that the enjoyable experience of goodness would pursue him all the days of his life – for at that moment he was still being chased by Absalom. And the last thing that you would think he could say about the coup d'état that had driven him from his palace was that it was a pleasant experience. If David was being pursued by hounds then they appeared to be of a pretty vicious type. But it is quite the contrary, says David, no matter how disappointing, frustrating, or depressing our experience is; if we are God's people then ultimately only good can come of every situation.

So, if the historical background of this psalm suggested by Professor E. M. Blaiklock and older scholars is true, this psalm is an amazing commentary on the words of Paul, that, '*In everything God works for good with those who love him, who are called according to his purpose.*' (Romans 8·28).

No one would want to be removed from power by his own son or go through the humiliation of having nothing with which to feed his family and supporters. Yet the amount of blessing that came through this painful experience was quite remarkable. Not only was this a time when David made a personal rediscovery of God, but he also had such a unique vision of *God as the Shepherd* that he had a message to pass on to people of countless generations. No wonder he could say that goodness would pursue him: he had learnt it the hard way.

The other word that David uses here is *mercy* – one of the great Old Testament words. No one has yet bettered *loving kindness*, which was Coverdale's translation; but while this expresses the *quality* of mercy it does not define its *quantity*. The point that David is making with this word is that God's mercy is *eternal*.

All hands to dance and skylark

David's whole life is a good illustration of the mercy of God, a mercy that is so eternal that it pursues in order to forgive and restore, time and time again. David's experience of it shows that eternal loving kindness of God in the life of someone who already knows him. But the inexorable nature of God's mercy in the life of an unbeliever can hardly be better illustrated than in the history of the *Mutiny on the Bounty*.

HMS *Bounty* under the command of Lieutenant Bligh left England in 1787, outward bound for the South Seas to collect bread-fruit trees. They landed at Tahiti in the Pacific and the crew spent the first few weeks enjoying the warm sea and the company of the Tahitian girls. The island girls were not only very attractive but were also so free with their favours that many of the sailors wanted to settle permanently on the island. Captain Bligh managed to call them back to their duties, and with a few grumbles they loaded the ship's cargo and set sail once more. On the 28th April 1789, only a few days out from Tahiti, the crew mutinied under the leadership of Fletcher Christian. Captain Bligh, together with eighteen loyal sailors, was set adrift in an open boat. They eventually reached Timor in the East Indies some 4,000 miles away, which is a miracle story in itself.

Meanwhile the mutineers had returned to Tahiti, where they managed to persuade twelve Tahitian girls to accompany them aboard the *Bounty* and set sail, with no other plans than to avoid capture. Their first landfall was Pitcairn

93

Island, an extinct volcano with steep cliffs in place of Tahiti's broad expanses of sand. It was uninhabited and had luscious vegetation so the mutineers decided to make it their new home. They took their own possessions and the contents of the *Bounty* ashore, then scuttled her by setting her alight. No one could now prove that they were the *Bounty* mutineers and they were free to establish the sort of life that they had begun to enjoy on Tahiti.

What they had planned to be their own version of heaven on earth proved to be a nightmarish hell which lasted for ten years. One of the men had taken the ship's copper kettle ashore and it was used to make spirits by distilling plant roots. The whole island was drunk for weeks on end. Some of the sailors went out of their minds, one committed suicide by jumping off a cliff, and all of them lived in a bestial way.

After several years there were only two men left, Alexander Smith and Edward Young. Edward Young, by far the older, was ill with asthma. Both these men had been forced to live apart from the women, who by capturing the men's firearms had moved to another part of the island with the eighteen children. The men were threatened with death if they followed. Edward Young knew that he was dying and in despair searched through his belongings to see if he could find anything that would remind him of the peace and the sanity of his early life in England. In the ship's chest he found the *Bounty*'s Bible and began to read. Alexander Smith could not read, so Edward Young decided to teach him by beginning at Genesis and going through each chapter word by word. By the time they reached Leviticus they were aware of their own need and had begun to pray. Before they reached the New Testament, Edward Young had died, but not before Smith had learned to read. For Alexander Smith, reading the New Testament meant the full discovery of peace, forgiveness and restoration.

Even at a distance the children had noticed the change in the living habits of the men, and soon the women and children had returned to see exactly what had happened. In 1808, nineteen years after the mutiny of the *Bounty* a ship from Boston discovered the community on Pitcairn Island. When the captain of the ship returned to America he took news of the only mutineer to survive and of what he called, 'the most perfect Christian society that he had ever seen'.

In the National Maritime Museum at Greenwich, there is a show case containing some of the relics of the *Bounty* which survived the first eighteen years on Pitcairn Island. There is also a card that comments on the religious revival which had swept through the island starting with the discovery of the ship's Bible. How well this story illustrates the pursuing mercy of God.

Life in the eighteenth century navy was harsh and there was always the possibility of mutiny. A captain on a long and tedious voyage would occasionally ask his bosun to pipe the order '*All hands to dance and skylark*'. That order gave the men absolute freedom to enjoy themselves. But the men of the *Bounty* never completely enjoyed themselves on Tahiti and certainly not on Pitcairn Island. The *dancing and skylarking*, the fun of life, was only discovered when man's need was met with the pursuing mercy of God.

The House of the Lord

Not only was David sure of God's pursuing goodness and mercy, but he was also certain that one day he would '*dwell in the house of the Lord forever*'.

As a shepherd gathers his flock into a fold, so David was sure that God would gather his people into the comfort and security of a homely atmosphere. If we ever imagine heaven as a house, it is very easy to fall into the trap of thinking of it as a cold and lifeless palace. The reverse is true. Although Jesus used the word '*house*' when he spoke about heaven, at least two New Testament scholars say that this word should be translated *caravanserai*,[5] that is, the hotel in the middle of the desert, the place where the traveller could find rest, refreshment and good company.

Have a nice forever

Some people find that the most disturbing thing about heaven is that it has no end. When I was ill recently some artist friends sent me a present. Instead of the usual get-well-soon card, they made me seven little badges, one for each day of the week. They were gay little badges with a slogan. My favourite was Sunday's badge, which said 'Have a nice forever'. And that is the most important thing about heaven, it is nice; it is not churchy or dull or formal, it is comfortable and homely. It is God's house. Going to heaven is like going on holiday to the nicest house that we know. The sad thing about most holidays is that they come to an end, while heaven will not.

So within the six short verses of this psalm, David discovers that God is *everything to him*. Although David's days are past, God has not changed at all. What David discovered about God is there for us all to find. We, too, can say *HE IS EVERYTHING TO ME*.

1. *Four Psalms* by Dr George Adam Smith, Hodder and Stoughton, page 33.
2. *A Shepherd Remembers* by Leslie Weatherhead, Hodder and Stoughton, page 195.
3. *The Land of the Book by* W. M. Thompson, Thomas Nelson and Sons Ltd.
4. *Woman at the Well* by Dale Evans, Oliphants, page 45.
5. *Readings in St John* by William Temple, Macmillan vol. 2, page 226
   Commentary on St John's Gospel by Dr Westcott, page 200-201.